Not

Taught

What It Takes to be Successful in the
21st Century that Nobody's Teaching You

JIM KEENAN

NOT
TAUGHT

—∞∞∞—

**WHAT IT TAKES TO BE SUCCESSFUL IN THE 21ST
CENTURY THAT NOBODY'S TEACHING YOU**

Jim Keenan

ISBN: 0692520767

ISBN 13: 9780692520765

To my three rockin' girls, Kenna, Elle and Ava.
I love you.
You move me.
Your energy is my energy.
You possess infinite talent, brilliance, beauty, creativity,
and brawn.
The world is yours.
Go crush it . . .

Daddy!!!

No one is telling you that what it takes to be successful has changed.

Until now.

Contents

Foreword

If Wishes Were Horses

I'M WRITING THIS from the inside of a factory. People used to weave textiles here that would be used for upholstering America's carriages. The building no longer serves that purpose, of course. It's a loft now, where creatives like me work and live. There are countless buildings like this all over the United States and other countries as well.

My friend James Altucher says if you wander around New York City looking at the big skyscrapers, most of the floors that used to house office workers are empty. We don't need to house everyone there any longer, because their jobs are all dried up.

We learned how to do more with fewer people.

The Big Pivot and a New Teacher

You know how people say, "there are two kinds of people?" There are millions of versions of two kinds of people.

Here's one: There are two kinds of people, those who keep hoping the past will come back, and those who equip themselves for the new normal.

This leads us to Jim Keenan.

Keenan (only people who don't know him call him Jim) is a bridger. He came from the same world you previously understood, where you went to work, did your job, went home, watched TV, and bought everything you could possibly buy, never worrying about whether you'd have a job.

But Keenan also knows every inch of the new world, where co-working spaces and coffee shops have replaced offices, where people always have more than one job, where work follows us around in a little glass rectangle in our pockets, and where you're doomed if you don't move fast to learn all the things that seem crazy and silly and childish.

SUCCESS HAS A NEW PATH

What Keenan teaches in this book is that you have to use all the new tools. If you're over 30, you're going to have to put on your "this isn't just for kids" mindset, and even though some of this seems really dumb (it does!), it's what will take you there.

Keenan is 47. I actually had to text him to ask that. You'd never know. He's got a vibrance and a youthful nature that really betrays the label of his age. But that's on purpose. He HAS to show you an exaggerated example of what you need to do so that you can really catch its importance.

Discomfort is Expected

One of the huge tenets of the book is that you have to become a kind of TV star. I'm using that term loosely, but it's close enough. Keenan points out that you have to become a bit more "known" and work on your **reach** via the online channel. We don't *trust* people who lack a digital footprint. We don't trust people who are invisible to this whole "selfie" culture.

And I know! I know this is bugging you. You're looking at these words and thinking, "there's nothing I want LESS than to think about taking photos of myself or being a YouTube personality." I know. I really do. My work is primarily with people ages 35-76 years of age (Except Cara, who is 83).

This is not about age. It's about accepting a new way of reaching out, finding the world you need for your business, and helping that world know more about you so that they'll want to do more business with you.

IF WISHES WERE HORSES, THEN BEGGARS WOULD RIDE

There's no one better to step you through this than Jim Keenan. He is not going to go slow. Jim is the ultimate Band-Aid ripper-offer. Fast! Ouch! Okay, now it's done.

I know you wish that you could do things they way you've always done them. But look at your bank account. Look at the rise in hours you're working. Look at the people losing their jobs all around you. Did YOU lose your job?

If you're all the way through the foreword, then you're one of three people (I've expanded to THREE!): you're either Keenan or you're someone who reads EVERY little bit of the book or you're really unsure what you're getting yourself into.

If you're that third kind, buy the damned book and learn something. I promise it'll help.

Chris Brogan
CEO, Owner Media Group

INTRODUCTION

WHAT IF I told you that your degree is less valuable today than it was twenty-five years ago? What if I told you that your professional experience doesn't mean a hill of beans in today's workforce? What if I told you that employers really don't care anymore how *hard* you work? That your most valuable asset isn't your house but your social media presence? That if you want to be successful in the twenty-first century, you have to become a thought leader? That if you can't sell, your chances to succeed are severely limited?

These things and more are *exactly* what I'm going to tell you in this book. *I'm going to teach you what no one has taught you.*

This book is going to shock you, frustrate you, and challenge everything you know about what it takes to be successful. I'm going to tell you what no one else is telling you—that the world has changed and the rules for success have changed with it. If you want to achieve success in this new world, you'll have to learn some new things. What we've been taught has become obsolete and gets more irrelevant as time goes by.

THINGS HAVE CHANGED

Haven't you noticed? Haven't you felt it? It's almost impossible not to have noticed. It's all around you.

Most of us can sense it. Something is going on, but you just can't put your finger on it. Your gut is telling you that things are different, but you're having trouble articulating it. Well, take solace in the fact that you're not crazy. And if you are feeling the changes, that's good. A lot of people haven't yet, and that will make what I say in this book that much harder to swallow.

The changes you're feeling, those little sensations in your gut telling you that the world is a different place than it was just a few years ago, are spot on. The world has changed, and it's a *big* change.

This book will prepare you to capitalize on this change and set yourself up for success. So what is this *big* change?

THE CHANGE OF AN ERA, AN *AGE*

We are moving into a new era. We're living through the change of an *age*. Let that sink in for a second.

This is a new era: brand-new in the history of the world. We've moved from the industrial age to the information age. This kind of change has happened only a handful of times in the history of human civilization. And we're living through it.

I know, right?! How crazy is that?

In human history, only a small group of us gets to experience such a shift. Before this one, the last major change was the onset of the Industrial Revolution 150 years ago. Back then we went from an agrarian society to an industrial one. Millions of people moved from self-sustaining farms and small plots of land into the city and into industrial jobs. Those who figured out how to manage this new industrial world won.

If you think that what it took to be successful in the agrarian age was what it took to be successful in the industrial age, you better be glad you weren't there. You would've been toast!

The most noticeable shift to success from an agrarian society to an industrial one had to do with education. If you wanted to crush it in the industrial age, you needed a formal education. This was *not* the case in an agrarian society. Learning to navigate in the new industrial age was critical to success, and those who figured it out won.

Some figured it out, and others didn't. Today is no different.

The industrial age began in the mid- to late 1800s and arguably stuck with us until right around the mid-1980s to early 2000s. Now just like education in the shift from the agrarian age to the industrial age, new rules and approaches to success in the information age are talking hold and becoming pervasive. We're ushering in a new era and with it new rules and approaches to success.

I'm here to tell you all about these new rules—the ones that aren't taught yet because they're still so new! You'll notice that much of what I'm writing is contrary to many of those cherished ideas about success that we, as an industrial and even post-industrial society, have held on to for so long. As we cast new systems, we are dismantling the old "conventional wisdom" that no longer serves us.

Some Things Haven't Changed

If I've successfully scared the shit out of you in the first few pages, rest easy. In spite of all the changes, some things haven't changed. When it comes to success, you're still going to have to work your ass off. There will never be a substitute for hard work, and the dawning of a new age isn't going to change that. Quite the contrary, hard work is going to be just as important now, if not more so, than it's ever been. Today, however, it's where you focus that hard work that matters.

Like hard work, grit and determination are still critical. If you don't have the fortitude to keep going, you won't make it. Drive, commitment, and hustle are as valuable today as they've always been—confidence and passion, too. You are going to need all you've ever had to be successful now. These characteristics are still must-haves. Those folks with crazy amounts of passion and confidence will benefit in the information age.

The difference in the information age will be where you focus your hard work, where you focus your grit and determination, what you're passionate about.

In spite of what hasn't changed, like the industrial age before it the information age demands that we develop new skills and traits. Knowing which ones is critical to getting ahead.

WHY CHANGE NOW?

How does moving from one age to the next change what it takes to be successful? Ages mark fundamental transitions in the way we live our lives. New ages mark major shifts in technology and social structure, which influence how we live, work, and play. And in this age shift, the change has been in the access to and the amount of information.

THE WORLD HAS BEEN BLOWN WIDE OPEN

Information is power. I know it's a cliché, but as it relates to the information age, it's an appropriate one.

The massive increase in the information available via the Internet has changed the playing field. It has created new distribution mediums, new teaching mediums, new engagement mediums, and more. The barriers to learning, growth, engagement, and interaction are gone. Information is no longer owned, guarded, or distributed by just a few.

We don't need a university or a teacher to access knowledge. Engagement has changed—we have access to those with power and prestige as they are tweeting, posting on Facebook, and engaging with us directly. There are fewer people, organizations, systems, or rules in our way because there are far fewer gatekeepers. Anyone can meet anyone else at any given time, anywhere in the world.

This avalanche of information and the eradication of gatekeepers have accelerated everything. Anything and anyone can be accessed. The world is wide open, and it's changing everything. Change is coming at a devastating pace, showing no mercy and wiping out those who choose to stand still.

THIS PACE OF CHANGE IS REDEFINING SUCCESS

Employers are no longer interested in robots (or as my friend Anthony Iannarino says, "Actually, they are interested in robots, and if you don't create value, you'll be replaced by one"). Companies are desperate for people who can create change, drive innovation, and think for themselves. Companies know they need independent employees who make things happen and don't need to be spoon-fed.

The world is changing and so are the rules.

Unfortunately, most organizations haven't adjusted yet. They haven't figured out what it's going to take to be successful in the information age. They know things are different. They know they need new skills, but they haven't solved the problem yet, and the victim of this is *you!*

You are not being taught the skills required to be successful in the information age. Our schools are not teaching our kids. They are learning on their own. We're all learning on our own, and the cost is devastating.

If You're over Thirty, You're in the Dark and No One Is Teaching You

It's not fair that no one is teaching you these keys to success. I wrote this book to change that. It will open your eyes to more than just the changes happening around you; it will show you what it's going to take to compete in this new era of information and frictionless communication.

You deserve to know what the playing field looks like. You deserve to know the new rules of the game.

If I'm successful in convincing you that the world has changed and the old paths to success are gone, *and* then you embrace the new keys to success, your world is going to look a whole lot different. You will have more opportunities at your disposal. You will know more people. More people will know you and seek you out. You will make more money. You'll never be unemployed. You'll have complete control over your situation and life. Your life will never again be made for you—you will be making your own life.

Read that paragraph again before you go any further. Isn't this what we all live for? Read it again, and if it's not what you want, you can put this book down. If you *do* want to make more money, have more relationships, and have greater control of your future and life, then keep reading. Your world is going to change.

Now what you do with this info is up to you. But at least when you're done with this book, you can't say you haven't been taught!

Let the teaching begin!

CHAPTER 1

REACH

Reach is arguably the most valuable non-monetary asset in the world.

MY REACH REVOLUTION

THE KEYS TO success in today's world addressed in this book are based on my own career and my study of many others who have risen to amazing heights because they, too, were early adopters of information age skills and traits, including Gary Vaynerchuk, who grew his family wine business from $3 million to $60 million in just five years, and Chris Brogan, who went from a small blogger in 1998 to an Internet celebrity, CEO, and highly sought after speaker. Their accomplishments are a testament to the power and value of these keys to success in the new age.

Although not as robustly, I too have benefitted from early adoption of these skills. I was a fast rising star. I enjoyed a meteoric rise in my career, going from salesperson to VP of sales. In just four years, I found myself responsible for a $300 million sales organization. My career was flying. Over time, however, I noticed my career starting to peak. It was outpacing my experience.

In other words, when it came time to compete with others for a senior executive sales leadership position, my competition had been around for fifteen, twenty, thirty years, whereas I had been around less than ten. I was having a hard time competing with that tenure. I learned this lesson the hard way after a merger when the majority of the incumbent sales team, including me, had to go.

Since I had such a stellar track record, I wasn't fazed at all. Surely I'd find a new job in a few months. I was wrong. It took almost a year to find a new position.

I said never again. The time away from work put a tremendous strain on my family and me. I had just gotten married. We had a baby, and I was building a new home. Being out of work that long was rough. Because of this hardship, I made a decision that changed my life forever— I started a blog.

I thought that if I could write every day about sales and sales leadership and how I had addressed the challenges that salespeople and leaders face regularly, I could build a decent-sized audience. My thinking was, if I ever needed a job again, all I had to do was announce it on my blog, and I'd have a few hundred or maybe even a few thousand people who could help out.

That was my logic. Little did I know what would happen next.

Within two years of writing religiously almost every day, people started noticing and reaching out. I started getting requests for help. People would reach out and say, "I read your post on…we need some help in that area. Can you help us?" I was getting requests for paid consulting. At first I was too busy with my full-time job, so I politely turned them down.

But then, out of nowhere, I was the victim of another merger—this one from overseas. Again, the majority of the local sales organization was let go, myself included.

After the layoff, I sat in my home office and asked myself, "Do I spend the next year looking for another job, *or* do I spend the next year trying to build a consulting practice leveraging the blog?" I chose the blog and called up the people who had reached out.

Within a few years of that decision, my A Sales Guy blog had become internationally known. I had clients in multiple countries and was regularly named as one of the most influential salespeople in the world. Today, I am asked to speak all around the country and have a thriving consulting practice. This is all from building tremendous reach through my blog, and then Twitter, LinkedIn, YouTube, and Instagram.

CREATE YOUR OWN REACH REVOLUTION

The world has gotten a lot bigger—not a little bigger, but a *lot!* The information age has brought together the four corners of the world in real time. Geographic boundaries have been virtually wiped out in less than ten years. You can now meet someone in almost every country in less than an hour via social media, email, or video. Meeting people is frictionless. It's never been easier to market to, connect with, and engage anyone, anywhere in the world in real time—that is, instantly. Like it or not, the business world has gone global, and this shift has created the greatest new opportunity for success ever.

THE SIZE AND REACH OF YOUR SPHERE OF INFLUENCE WILL DETERMINE YOUR SUCCESS

To be successful in the information age, you need to be able to reach a boatload more people than you did during the industrial age. You need a really fucking big network or digital Rolodex if you want to kill it in the twenty-first century. Those who cannot cultivate a massive audience with tremendous influence or reach are doomed! When I say really fucking big, I mean thousands, tens of thousands, and even hundreds of thousands.

I can see the contorted faces now as you process this idea of reaching thousands and thousands of people, and why it matters. Let me break it down.

Reach Is Worth Billions of Dollars—That's Billions with a "*B*"

At the turn of the twentieth century, one of the wealthiest men in the world was William Randolph Hearst. His worth was entirely built on reach. Starting in 1887, Hearst built the country's largest newspaper empire, which included *The San Francisco Examiner*, *The New York Journal*, and others. By the time he completed his acquisitions, he controlled nearly thirty newspapers. He then moved into magazines. In the end, Hearst built the largest media company in the world. Yes, the world!

That's a helluva a reach!

Newspapers are useless if no one buys them, if no one is reading them. Newspapers require eyeballs to be successful: eyeballs, subscribership, access, reach. The bigger the reach, the more valuable the paper.

William Randolph Hearst could reach millions and millions of people. He could reach more people than anyone else in the world at the time. That's why he was one of the richest men in the world.

With the Exception of Oil and Banking, *Reach* Is the Most Valuable Asset Today

Why do some athletes make more money in endorsements than they do in salary from their sport? Why do some entertainers make more money from their endorsements than from movie and TV income? Why is it that some of the most valuable companies in the world during the industrial age were media companies, like CBS, NBC, and ABC?

Why? Because all of these people and companies have reach. They can reach right into our hearts and minds through TV, newspaper, and radio. They capture our attention and we welcome them into our living rooms, breakfast nooks, drive time—our lives.

Reach is big money. Those with the most, win. People and companies pay for reach and pay handsomely.

HIS AIRNESS

Michael Jordan is one of the most powerful examples of the value of reach. Michael hasn't played basketball in over a decade, yet his image—you know the one, him flying through the air toward the basket—is still printed on all kinds of Nike apparel. Michael's reach, his ability to influence the purchase of sports clothing, is unmatched even though he hasn't shot a basketball as a professional in twelve years. His reach has extended his financial gains and success beyond his playing years simply because his image and name influence millions of people to the tune of hundreds of millions of dollars.

REACH DIDN'T USED TO BE FOR THE AVERAGE JOE

From the industrial age all the way up to the time when the Internet began making information available to the masses, creating reach was difficult and expensive. Reach was big business and was guarded like gold. Those who had it knew it and levied a tax on everyone who wanted it. If you wanted reach, whether as a private individual or a big company, you either paid for it (advertising) or tried to create it. And creating reach then was a difficult thing to do.

Back then the only way to create your own reach was to start your own publishing or media company. But that was expensive and the competition was tough. Competing with incumbents like CBS, NBC, *The New York Times*, or even your local paper was almost impossible, even with huge piles of cash.

You could become famous—that would create reach. You could become a famous athlete, a famous actor, or novelist. But even then you had to rely on the entrenched media—the agents, radio stations, TV stations, movie studios, publishing houses, and others.

They were the gatekeepers, carefully guarding access to their networks *and* meticulously crafting the image of those who were granted access. Therefore, even if you were able to become famous, in many cases, someone else managed your success and the access to your network. Building your own reach on your own terms was almost impossible.

A Funny Thing Happened on the Way to the Information Age

The rise of the information age began to change things. The incumbents began to lose their foothold as the

Internet made access available to the masses. People no longer needed the paper, the radio, or even the TV to get their word out. Regular people could go straight to masses through YouTube, MySpace, Facebook, Vimeo, blogging, Twitter, and more. Little by little, the Internet created new ways for us to connect with others and tell our story without having to go through the juggernaut of traditional media. We no longer need "permission."

Circumventing the gatekeepers has democratized reach and opened it to the rest of us. We have choices now. Choices eradicate consolidation and monopolies.

Books can be best sellers without publishers. Music sensations can sell millions of records without record labels. Movies can be created without a studio. The middle man, the agent, the "gatekeeper" is being marginalized.

That means that traditional media forums have been getting their asses handed to them. Newspapers, magazines, and others are losing the battle of reach. We've all read the stories of the failing print industry. The Internet broke their lock on eyeballs and, with that, their revenue stream.

Everyone can now build, develop, and engage their own personal network on any topic based on their own knowledge, talent, and expertise. That's a big deal.

Let me say that again. That's a *big* deal...that anyone who aims to be successful in the information age should be capitalizing on.

The Long Tail

In 2006, Chris Anderson published *The Long Tail*. In it, he talks about how the Internet has created more consumer choice by eliminating constraints on physical space. That is, before the Internet, stores could only carry so many products because they only had so much shelf space. This limited carrying capacity forced them to sell only the most popular items.

If an item didn't move fast enough, it wasn't stocked because it was too expensive to stock or sell anything that sat on the shelf too long, not generating revenue. This scarcity of shelf space limited consumer choice. Millions of products and services were not available to the public or had to be found through specialty stores.

When the Internet came along, shelf space became irrelevant. Companies didn't need shelf space to display and peddle their goods. The cost of inventory came way down, as the cost of storage was next to nil. More and more obscure products could be offered. Therefore, artists, creators, authors, and other content creators didn't have to compete to get access to the public. They could create their own website or join sites like Etsy.

The public was no longer stuck with just the top 10 percent of the most popular items. We finally got access to the most obscure, unique, and niche items imaginable.

THE LONG TAIL

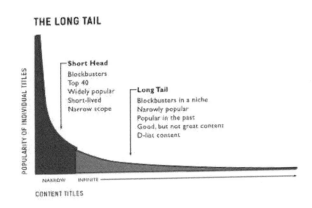

Before the information age, most of what was available to us was in the *short head,* as shown in the graphic above, because it was too expensive to offer us things in the *long tail.* Thanks to the information age, much of what we buy today is in the long tail, like your nephew's garage band releases, your aunt Mildred's quilts, and your weird uncle's self-published sci-fi book. Cumulatively, the long tail is bigger than the short head.

This long-tail effect can also be seen in digital online media. Anyone can post a video on YouTube of themselves singing. Anyone can post articles or create their own on-line "newspaper" instantly for pennies. Photographers can upload their photos to Flickr for free. All of these sites have given us access to artists, writers, bands, singers, actors, thought leaders, and others to whom we *never* would have had access before.

This has resulted in a slow, but definitive, dismantling of the old guard's control of reach, and it's been transformational over the past ten years. It's created Internet sensations and introduced us to new talents and ways of thinking and being in the world.

It's been a boon for all of us. We've been the lucky beneficiaries of more choice.

Learning to play in this space is critical for success in the twenty-first century. Because of this access, you must be able to influence more people than those you work with or live near. If you can't, *you're in trouble.*

WE'RE WARY OF PEOPLE WHO ARE DIGITALLY ANONYMOUS

Digitally anonymous refers to people who are unknown online, have no digital presence, or do not exist or barely exist online. If the people at your company, in your neighborhood, and in your physical in-real-life network are the only people who know how good you are, *you're screwed.*

We've become so accustomed to finding, watching, reading, and engaging with people online that we've come to expect that those with value—those who know their shit— are online. We're wary of those who aren't. We're wary of people without LinkedIn profiles, and it's become increasingly unacceptable not to be found in a Google search.

Recently, a sales leader told me she wouldn't even look at a resume of a person who doesn't have a picture on their LinkedIn profile and at least five hundred connections. She doesn't care how good their work experience is. The recruiters at my recruiting company, A Sales Guy

Recruiting, won't submit a candidate if they don't have a picture. It has become evident that if you don't have a minimum online presence, you are falling behind.

BUILD YOUR REACH ASSET

Reach is no longer the asset of a few, no longer a tool reserved for the wealthy or those carefully chosen by the gatekeepers. Reach is now an asset available to anyone who is committed to building it, cultivating it, and protecting it.

If you want to crush it, if you want to rise to greater heights in your career, you're going to have to grow your reach. Start thinking about how you can build an audience of thousands, not tens. Start creating a social media presence that will capture the attention of those in your space and establish you as a reliable, valuable, credible resource. Build an audience who knows you, respects you, and follows you because of the value you bring to your space. Without them, success will be very difficult to achieve.

CONNECTING WITH PEOPLE IN MEANINGFUL WAYS HAS NEVER BEEN EASIER

Think about it: the Internet and the mobile phone have erased all barriers to connecting and, therefore, to success. In fact, Facebook recently released research showing that instead of the infamous "Kevin Bacon standard" of six degrees of separation between us, there are now only *3.74 degrees.* That means the entire world is only "a friend of a friend" away from you!

Endless possibilities open up for people who see this new world with eyes wide open. If you can hustle, if you know how to connect with people in a genuine way, if you have real knowledge to share, you can write your own ticket.

THE DIGITAL ROLODEX

It's all you. Your online presence is your key to the kingdom. Establish yourself as a thought leader, demonstrate your expertise and knowledge, and reach out to help others along the way. By consistently fostering real connections and sharing value, you will build a support system that will respond when you need it. The people in your growing circle will have your back because you have theirs. You have earned their trust over time through your online living resume and presence.

People use social networking tools to figure out who they can trust and rely on for decision making. By the end of this decade, power and influence will shift largely to those people with the best reputations and trust networks, from people with money and nominal power. That is, peer networks will confer legitimacy on people emerging from the grassroots.

—Craig Newmark, Founder of Craigslist

Your online presence—whether you call it your social graph or amplified reach—has a direct impact on your life. In 2009, I said that your social graph would one day be worth more than your home, and I meant it.

During the Great Recession, one of the only ways to get a job was to know someone. There were too many people competing for too few jobs. Without a personal connection, getting a job was next to impossible. Today the economy is better, but it is still true that who you know helps you get better opportunities faster. But now you can "know" someone over Twitter, Vine, LinkedIn, Facebook, or your blog comments. These weak-tie connections, as Stanford sociologist Mark Granovetter named them in the seventies, have become more meaningful than many of our strong tie connections in terms of actually making things happen.

LIVE FROM NEW YORK…LEVERAGING AROUND-THE-WORLD REACH

In 2013, the owner of the influential Facebook Page and now book of the same name *Humans of New York* (HONY), Brandon Stanton, was able to turn a simple photo into enough money for *his driver to bring home a second adopted child in just sixty minutes!* This was all because HONY had built a strong online community by offering sincerity, knowledge, and value with every interaction. By bridging the gap between the computer and the people on the other side of the screen, Stanton changed someone's life for the better. His strong social graph also got him that book deal. This story is amazing on its own, but what is even more amazing is that *we all* have that power.

We have never been more in control of our destinies than we are right now.

If you think I'm joking, take a look at Sarah Cortes's story. She was injured in rural New York and then taken to a hospital in Pennsylvania. That hospital wanted to perform extensive spinal surgery against her will. Through the power of Twitter and her strong social graph, she managed to avoid a completely unnecessary surgery. For another example of the power of our weak-tie connections, look at how cancer survivors rally around each other and create support, success, and financial help through networks like #BCSM.

WE WERE MADE TO CONNECT WITH ONE ANOTHER

The online and mobile world simply amplifies that natural drive, giving it deeper meaning and easier access. If your sphere is small, you can't influence large amounts of people through social media and you're not optimized for the information age.

The key is to be seen as active, engaged, and generous on social media. Then you will get noticed. With notice comes reach, and with reach comes influence, and I cannot undersell the importance of influence to success in the twenty-first century.

SOCIAL MEDIA IS A *MUST*

As much as it may or may not pain you, you need to get on Twitter, Pinterest, LinkedIn, Instagram, Facebook, and the other channels that make sense for your niche. You have to leverage social media to engage, share, and connect with people like you in your industry and areas of interest. Share their tweets and blog posts. Engage them in LinkedIn groups and on Quora. Curate content you find around the web that is consistent with your brand and area of expertise. Create content; start a blog or post on LinkedIn. Ask and answer questions on Twitter, Quora, and LinkedIn groups. Create a YouTube channel.

No matter what you do, no matter your profession, your expertise, or your hobby, nothing will be more instrumental in the development of your success than your ability to influence a large swatch of people quickly—your reach. Reach is the cornerstone, the foundation of success in the twenty-first century. Start building yours now.

CHAPTER 2

BRAND YOU

It's not OK to be anonymous.

As I SAID in the previous chapter, if no one knows who you are, you're in deep shit. Digital obscurity will be the plague of the commoner in the information age. If you live in digital obscurity, you are losing the race. Not only are you losing, you're falling further and further behind every day. If the only people who know you or know that you're badass are your friends, family, neighbors, coworkers, and college and high school acquaintances, you are setting yourself up for perfect failure.

Being known *only* by those people you've met in person no longer suffices. You now have to have a global digital brand that resonates with everyone who comes into contact with it.

Digital obscurity is a death sentence, long and slow. It creeps up on you year by year, only causing severe damage when you find yourself in need of a new job or other help from your network.

When You Google Yourself, What Happens?

Are you on the first page? Second page? Third page? Oh God, please tell me you're at least on the third page!

If you're not, you don't exist online. And if you don't exist online, you don't exist to 99.999 percent of the world. And I promise, if you want to be successful in today's world, that's a problem.

If you expect to find what you're looking for every time you search Google, then you can bet your ass, so does everyone else—and that includes finding you!

Here's the Deal: You Are a Product

Yup! Accepting this premise now will save you a world of hurt because it is essential in your journey toward success. Like all products, you have to have a value proposition, a target market that embraces that value proposition, and most importantly, an identity or brand for which that product is known.

Without a brand, products die on the shelf. No one picks them up and puts them in their grocery cart. No one tells their friends about them. Products without a brand don't have raving fans. They don't sell and that is a problem.

If you want to be successful in today's world, you need to create *brand you* and promote the shit out of it.

Branding yourself is a deliberate effort in understanding the value you deliver, the approach you take to your craft, the impact you have in shaping your craft, and the outcomes you successfully achieve. Success is becoming increasingly more difficult to achieve without a well-developed personal brand.

Be Deliberate in Developing and Managing Your Career and Brand

It wasn't too long ago that most of us didn't consider branding ourselves. We were leaves in the wind, reacting to whatever job opportunities came our way or felt good. It wasn't uncommon not to give a single thought to who we were as an employee, as a deliverer of services, or as a product. We showed up at our job, did what was expected of us, and went home. We sold ourselves via our resume and our network.

Managing our career as if we were a product never entered our mind.

Many of the other must-have keys to success in this book are quickly becoming table stakes, but personal branding, or *branding you*, still provides tremendous opportunity and competitive advantage. There *is* real first mover advantage here. In today's world, you can still move through your career without a solid personal brand strategy. It's not yet mandatory. But it's not going to stay this way for much longer. Now is the time to act.

WE GOOGLE EVERYTHING!

As a society, we are in constant need of information about the people, ideas, places, and things in our lives. This need for more and more information has created an unexpected knee-jerk reaction—*we don't trust the things we can't find in Google.*

We've become information addicts. Searching the Internet and Googling are our default actions. When was the last time you bought something without looking it up online first? Aside from the weekly groceries, we Google almost everything we buy. If we want to learn about something or someone, the very first thing we do is Google it!

We Google everything and everybody, from our first date to our new nanny, from famous people to new cars we want to buy. We Google the companies where we're interviewing while they're Googling us and the other candidates they'll be interviewing. We Google our kids' teachers, the new neighbors moving in, and the book our friend just told us was awesome.

DIGITAL ANONYMITY CREATES DISTRUST

If we can't or don't find information about something online, we don't trust it. We are left wondering, "Hmmm, why can't I find this company, person, or product online? What's up with that?"

We check out and move away from it. Doubt has set in, trust has been violated, fear has entered the equation, and we don't buy when fear is involved. We don't buy or trust what we can't Google…and that includes *you*.

BUILDING *BRAND YOU* ENSURES THIS DOESN'T HAPPEN TO YOU

Building *brand you* ensures you're not anonymous because you can be found. What's more, it ensures that you are associated with the industry, ideas, and people that align best with you and the value you bring to the table. Building *brand you* makes it perfectly clear to prospective employers, customers, and industry peers who you are, what they get for working with and for you, what you represent, how you think, how you operate, and what you deliver for them. It removes the guessing game.

Building *brand you* and launching yourself from obscurity requires that you know:

1. Who you are, what you bring to the table, and what differentiates you.
2. The value you deliver to the people you impact.
3. Your target market, those to whom your value proposition provides the greatest value. If you don't know who will benefit from the value of your brand, then nothing else matters.

You Have to Understand the Product Features of *Brand You*

Building a killer personal brand starts with defining who you are, what skills you have, which services you offer, what expertise you possess, and what you are passionate about. The question you need to answer is: "What makes me different from every other teacher, accountant, salesperson, real estate agent, software developer, VC, mortgage broker, writer, marketer, operations executive, or whoever?"

Without this differentiation, you have nothing. You're average, and average ain't gonna win the race.

- You need to take your time with this and dig deep. There is no room for humility here.
- Ask your coworkers, bosses (former and present), friends, and relatives for help with this. What do they say about your brand? How do they evaluate your expertise? What do they say makes you better at what you do than everyone else? What do they say you're terrible at?
- Look at your body of work. How does it stack up to others? Be honest. Is it better? How? What makes it unique? What makes your body of work impressive?
- Measure yourself against others in your space. Are you better than they are? Why? In what ways? What do you do differently? What is your competitive differentiator?

Be honest and accurate in your self-assessment. If it sucks, admit it. At least you can fix it. If it's great, be proud and don't let false modesty dumb it down. Once you answer these questions, ask yourself, "What does all this provide others? What's my value proposition?"

Your Value Proposition

OK, now we're gonna flip the script. We've just spent all this time talking about you, who you are, and what makes you great, but now it's time to consider your audience—the people and companies to whom you deliver value.

What I'm about to tell you is the secret to success in all aspects of life.

It's the juice that makes everything flow. It's at the core of every transaction, every millionaire, every billionaire, and every relationship. Whether or not you're conscious of it is irrelevant. It is the key to success, because without it, there is no success. Get ready, you're gonna want to highlight this or jot it down or put it in Evernote, because you don't ever want to forget it.

The Secret to Success Is Creating *Value*!

That's it, y'all. It's that simple. The more value you bring to people or companies, the more successful you will be. Period.

I know you'd like to think the secret to success in life would be more sophisticated, more complex than that. It's not.

The simple truth is, value drives everything. Gold has value, stocks have value, our relationships have value, our families have value, our time has value, the companies we work for have value, the neighborhoods we live in have value, the corner pizza shop has value, and the woods you hike in, the path you run in the morning, and the book you read before you fell asleep last night all have value.

Everything has value, and the more value something has, the more in demand it is.

Value is at the core of every decision we make. Value is what drives where we live, where we work, how we spend our time, where we go to school, our decision *not* to go to school, what our major is, where we spend our vacation, how many kids we have, how much time we spend in the gym, and our choice to eat like shit. It's all driven by value—perceived value.

I'm Not Talking about Money Here

Don't get me wrong—money plays a big role. Money weaves itself into the value equation more often than not, but money is not true value.

Value is measured not by how badly you want something, but rather by what you're willing to give up for it.

Think about it. Value is rooted in what people are willing to part with in order to get what it is they want. That can be everything from money to time, relationships, dreams, careers, travel, experiences, and so on.

Life is a constant bartering game, where we as the participants trade one thing for another to create the life we want. We trade time for dollars. We trade work for family. We trade family for work. We trade fun for school. We trade school for fun. We trade money for vacations. We trade relationships for careers. We trade couches for health. We trade health for couches. We trade comfort for risk. We trade opportunity for security. We are constantly bartering in our lives, trading one thing for another, all in hopes of living the life we desire.

At the core of each and every one of those "transactions" is a perception of value. We ask ourselves if it's worth trading "this" for "that." Our answer to this question lies open and exposed, hinging on one thing: perceived value. If we see the value, we move. If we don't see the value, we protect the status quo. It's that simple.

Given this, you have to ask yourself, "What is my value to others, to my company, to my family, to my friends, to my coworkers, to the world? What value do I bring? What am I worth trading for?"

If you need help finding your answer, go back to the section about understanding the product features of *brand you* and use your description of self to create value.

- What is it you deliver to those around you?
- What does a company get from you?
- What makes you great?
- How does that benefit the companies and people who pay you to get shit done?

- How do you do things differently than others, and how does that increase your value?
- How is an organization changed because of your presence?
- Where do you create impact in the environments you engage?
- How are things different *after* you leave?

WHAT IS YOUR KING MIDAS EFFECT?

What is the effect of your presence, effort, commitment, engagement, attitude, intellect, creativity, and collaboration on your environment? In other words, what happens to the things you touch? Do they turn to gold?

In *Seven Habits of Highly Successful People*, Steven Covey used these questions to describe his second habit, that is, "begin with the end in mind":

- What do you want people to say about you at your funeral?
- How do you want to be remembered?
- What words would they use to describe you?

These powerful questions force us to define how we want to live our lives and the effect we want to have on people. The questions pull back the blinds to see clearly what it is we have to do in order to have people say what we want them to say about us at our funeral. That, my friend, is the King Midas effect in action.

Imagine answering these questions in a business setting:

- What do you want people to say about you after you leave your company?
- How do you want to be remembered by your co-workers and bosses?
- What words would you want them to use?

Your answers will be tremendously helpful as guiding principles to develop your brand. Building your value proposition is no different than asking what you want people to say about you at your funeral. You're just not looking that far down the road. You're looking at the here and now.

- What do you want people to say about who you are and what you get done in your career, job, or profession?
- Do you innovate?
- Do you drive more revenue?
- Are you more creative?
- Do you create change?
- Do you bring people together?
- Do you create relationships?
- Do you create stability?
- Do you ensure compliance?

- Are you able to fire people up?
- Do you uncover unseen opportunities?
- Are you a math genius?
- Do you combine several of these traits into being a super programmer, sales leader, marketer, recruiter, accountant, or something else entirely?

When you understand the impact you have on people and companies, you will know your value proposition. The bigger it is, more valuable it is and the more success you will reap.

TO BUILD *BRAND YOU*, YOU NEED TO BE DELIBERATE

Know your King Midas effect and what you turn into gold. Discover and develop your value proposition—one that delivers enormous value and is in demand. Deliver more than expected to the right people at the right time. Then make sure everyone else knows, too.

In today's ever-connected world, people are constantly on the lookout for value. They want to know what they get from you, why engaging with you is worth their time or money, and why they should pick you over someone else.

It's up to you to tell them and then show them. Building and promoting *brand you* makes that happen.

CHAPTER 3

CREATE CONTENT

A blog, YouTube, a podcast...it doesn't
matter.

You NEED TO start creating content. I'm simply going to say it. You have to. There is no shortcut. There is no exception. You must establish a way to create content in a blog, via a podcast, through a YouTube channel, using LinkedIn Pulse, or through any other medium. You get to choose. Choose any platform you want. Pick the one that best fits your personality and style, but pick you must. Not doing it is not an option. Creating content is your way to demonstrate to the world how good you are at what you do. You have to create content in the twenty-first century if success is your goal.

I Started with a Blog

I was helping my wife wash the dishes, and as we were finishing up, I told her I needed to write a blog post before I went to bed. At the time, I had been blogging for about a year. As I was putting the last dish away, my wife asked why I bothered with blogging. "What do you think you're going to get from doing that? How are you going to make any money?"

I could hear the contempt and disdain in her voice. She didn't get it and felt it was a waste of time that took me away from her and the family for a couple of hours each day. To be honest, I wasn't sure exactly what I was going to get out of it either. But I knew that documenting my knowledge and expertise on a regular basis couldn't be a bad thing.

And I was right! Through my blog I built a following of tens of thousands that, in essence, launched my company, A Sales Guy Consulting and Recruiting.

Creating Content Is a Force Multiplier When It Comes to Success

Think about sharing your knowledge like advertising. The content you create and share is the way you highlight to the world what you know and how competent you are. Content builds your intellectual repository—a bank for your ideas and insight. It is where and how you establish credibility for what you know, what you've learned over the years, and what you are continuing to learn.

In addition to credibility, your content provides visibility and engagement while at the same time increasing awareness, knowledge, and understanding of *you!* Content is the fuel that powers almost all of the other traits in this book. Of all the keys to success, if you commit to creating content regularly, you will demonstrate, deepen, and drive your mastery of many of the other keys to success, like thinking, accepting change, developing expertise, and branding yourself.

Content Takes the Pressure Off

In an age where information rules the day, not creating content leaves you on the outside looking in. Google rules our lives. We don't bring new people, products, or services into our lives without first doing a Google search.

Your content makes sure that the Google search is your best frickin' friend. When people search for content in your field, they need to find you. They need to find your expertise, your knowledge, and your value, not that of your competitors…or even worse, to find nothing at all!

Your content lets your ideas, knowledge, thoughts, perspective, and narratives tell your story. It is the most powerful way to attract new employers, customers, partners, and collaborators. Content is a living mouthpiece for what you know, how you do your job, what you are passionate about, and how you live your life.

Develop Yourself as an Expert

Regardless of what you choose to write about, your content will be far more impactful than anything you can say in an interview or first encounter. People are desperate for information. They don't like guessing. They don't like taking risks. They want to know as much as they can before they make a decision. People want data, and content is data about you. It's your ideas, insight, knowledge, expertise, and genius in easily digestible chunks.

When you create content, you take the risk out of the evaluation equation. You let your readers get comfortable with the idea of you as a thought leader and an expert before they meet you. Strong, substantive content backed with passion will become a critical tool to your success and personal growth. The key is to choose the right topic and, like all tools, know what you're going to use it for.

What Type of Content Should You Create?

The answer to this question is simple. There are basically two things to consider.

1) What are you passionate about?
2) Whose attention do you want?

The second is more important. If you're creating content and *no one* is reading, watching, or listening to it, then it's a hobby and it isn't going to contribute to your success. Yet writing what you're passionate about will contribute to your happiness, so everyone take a step back.

I'm not saying don't follow your passion if it doesn't have an audience. I am saying that your success will be more probable if you can combine your passion with an audience. Figure out a way to get in the middle of this figure, and you'll crush it.

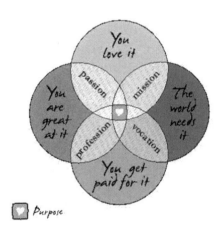

Purpose

What or Who Do You Want to Influence?

That's what we're talking about here—influence. Picking your topic starts with understanding what you want your blog, video, podcast, or other content to do and who you want to influence. Once you know where you want to go, what your journey will be, what you want your content to do, and who you want to impact, you'll know your topic. Ask yourself these questions:

- What are you passionate about?
- What do you love?
- What do you have to share with the world?
- What can the world learn from you?
- What are you good at?
- What does the world need?
- What type of content do you want to consume?

Answer these questions, and you'll find your way to the sweet spot at the center of all those circles. That's where your true content success is going to come from.

I know that when someone asks such a profound question like, "What can the world learn from you?" it can seem daunting and overwhelming. And that's exactly why creating content is so valuable. It forces you into the game. It doesn't let you sit on the sidelines. Once you commit, you have no choice but to play and play big.

So pick something and run with it. Don't wait. If it's in the middle of the circles, you can't pick wrong.

CREATING CONTENT IS A JOURNEY: WHERE DO YOU WANT IT TO TAKE YOU?

Make no mistake—your content will take you somewhere. Once you commit to a blog, a podcast, or videos, it's like paving a road while you're driving on it. It's taking you on a journey, so know where you want to go.

- Do you want to use it to accelerate your career?
- Do you want to use it to write a book?
- Do you want to use it to save dogs? (This is for Lisa, my friend whose stubborn ass refuses to start a blog for saving "bully" breeds. She'd be famous now if she had just frickin' listened to me. More importantly, she would have saved thousands of more dogs than she's saved to date.)
- Do you want to start a blog to help terminally ill people?
- Do you want create a podcast to protect gun rights?
- Do you want to create a video channel to help people manage their finances?
- Do you want to create a how-to blog to help people fix cars?

The options are infinite—you just have to get going.

CREATING CONTENT IS A LIFELONG COMMITMENT

Once you start, there is no stopping. Blogs, YouTube channels, and podcasts are dynamic living organisms. Once you stop writing, shooting, or recording, they die. Sometimes they die a slow death and sometimes it's immediate, but die they will. Content has a shelf life. Once you build an audience, they rely on you for more. They get greedy. They're going to want more and more from you. This is good, but it's daunting. Therefore, the key to creating content is to make sure you don't stop—ever.

I know that committing to something for the rest of your life is a monumental task, but you need to think of a blog, a YouTube channel, or a podcast as an asset. Like any other asset, they require care and feeding. Carefully tended content gains value over time. The longer you create new and fresh content, the more valuable the content becomes.

Be a Reliable Content Creator

If creating content is a lifetime commitment, you have to make it work for you. If you decide to blog or create a video or podcast every day, you may be setting yourself up for failure. Creating a blog post or video every day is a tremendous commitment, one few people can keep up with. Taking on that kind of commitment too early could be the very reason you fail. Too many people take on more than they can handle, and after a few months or even weeks, they get overwhelmed and quit.

To infuse content creation into your life, don't worry about the frequency. Rather focus on the consistency. Create a blogging schedule you can live with. Three times a week, once a week, two times a month, once a month—it doesn't matter. What matters is that you stick to your schedule.

It's more important that readers know *when* you'll be creating new content, when they should expect a new post, podcast, or video, rather than knowing how much content you'll create. Readers will adjust to your schedule if they know when you're creating. Be consistent.

ALL ABOUT THAT CONTENT

If consistency is how you build your content audience, frequency is the fertilizer. The more frequently you post and the more content you offer readers, the faster your audience will grow. Frequency of content accelerates the growth of your audience—the more content, the more often the search engines pick up your posts, the more searches you come up in, and so the more people can find you.

Build a schedule that allows you to post as often as possible but one that you can commit to for a very long time. Pick a frequency that works for you and just go for it. If you're not sure what you can do, start with once a week. That's a good cadence. Then go from there.

Whatever you do, don't stress about it! Creating fresh, informative, engaging content should be fun.

JUST GET CREATING

Now that you've committed to creating content, you've figured out the topic of the content, and you've nailed down your frequency, it's time to get going. But what to write, shoot, or talk about?

Aha! That's the million-dollar question, isn't it?

The good news is, it's *your* blog. Write, talk, or shoot whatever you want, keeping your audience in mind. Ask yourself what you want the audience to get from your posts.

When I sit down to write, I ask myself, "What are we gonna do today? Are we gonna teach, challenge, inspire, educate, or motivate?" I pick a topic that will accomplish one or more of those objectives.

Regardless of your topic, a video, blog post, or podcast that accomplishes anyone of these will be a good one.

Start Getting Ideas to Come to You

Once you've determined the objective of your post, decide on the topic. The best way I've found to come up with topics is to read a lot. The more I read about sales, sales leadership, selling, sales team development, and so on, the more ideas come to me. Reading triggers new thoughts and ideas to write about. Reading gives me things to challenge, espouse, and share.

In addition to reading, I now look at everything like, "This could be a good blog post." With clients, I'm thinking about how what we're working on could be a good blog post. I'm asking myself how many other companies could be struggling with this same issue. It might be something others would like to address. When I watch TV, listen to podcasts, and attend sales conferences and other professional development activities, I'm looking for my next blog post idea.

Every environment can be inspiration for a video, podcast or blog post. You just have to be looking. Start reading, follow other blogs in your space, create a Twitter stream around your topic, participate in LinkedIn groups, and hang out on Quora. Listen to the questions people are asking, and create posts that answer their questions. There is always something you can be talking about.

Over the past six years, I've written more than fourteen hundred blog posts. People like Seth Godin and Fred Wilson have written more than three or even four thousand posts. If you commit, there will be no shortage of topics and content you can share with your readers.

CONTENT CREATION IS A MUST-HAVE INVESTMENT

Without question, creating content is the most time-consuming and daunting key to success in the information age. It takes work, it can be hard, and it's not a quick fix. Yet when you have fifty, five hundred, a thousand, and more relevant, challenging, inspiring, educating posts, videos, podcasts, e-books, or LinkedIn Pulse posts with *your* name all over them—that gets people's attention!

Imagine being in a job interview and someone asks your perspective on something. You can say, "I wrote a post on that. I believe…" That sets you up to win.

Everyone who is serious about success needs to create content. It's really that simple. Get creating…then you'll know you're serious.

Video, Blog, Podcast…Oh My?

I'm sure many of you are asking, "How do I know what medium I should choose? Should I start a blog? Should I start a YouTube channel? Should I start a podcast? What is the best option?"

There is no right or wrong when it comes to the distribution platform. YouTube, WordPress, podcasts, and so on are just the delivery platforms. Therefore, the best way to determine which route to go is to ask yourself what fits your unique strengths best? Are you better with the pen than on camera? Are you an orator and find that speaking is a better way to get your points across? Are you a dramatic and energetic person who would crush it on video? Deciding on what medium to choose is personal and starts with you and your personality.

Pick the medium that best fits your strength, personality, and style. That's the one that will crush it. Don't over think it. Just go!

CHAPTER 4

CHANGE

The world has sped up in the past twenty years. The need to move fast is a requirement and yet, the rate of change is so rapid that it's difficult for companies to stay nimble enough to keep pace with market demands.

—JIM MCGINNIS, VICE PRESIDENT AT INTUIT

CHANGE HAPPENS

AND IT'S HAPPENING faster than it's ever happened before. There has never been a time in our history where change has been so prevalent. The information age has ushered in unprecedented change and, more importantly, unprecedented *rates* of change. Just twenty-five years ago, there was no Google, no Groupon, no Facebook, no Amazon, no YouTube, no eBay, and no Skype. Billion dollar corporations like BlackBerry had been born, dominated the marketplace, and subsequently died in that time. (Let it be known, Blackberry is still a functioning company, but are a speck of their original self. Once the 800 pound gorilla, they are no long relevant in the mobile phone arena.)

We've gone from a world where we were tethered to our homes by a telephone cord and a TV to a world where almost everyone has a mobile device and is accessible everywhere and at any time. Think about that. We went from a world of answering machines and scheduled programming to a world where we are turning the lights to our home off from a hotel five thousand miles away and watching our favorite shows from wherever we want, whenever we want, using only our phones. It's incredible! The rate of change over the past twenty-five years is like nothing we've ever experienced.

And here's the kicker—it's only getting faster. Change is accelerating, like a snowball rolling down a mountain. It's gaining speed and snow, barreling over anything and anyone in its way. In 1958, the average tenure for a company on the Standard and Poor's 500 was sixty-one years. In 1980, it was twenty-five years. Today, it is eighteen years. Today, billion dollar companies, like Groupon, are created in less than two years.

Ask Blackberry, Nokia, or Nortel about change. They'll tell ya what happens when you can't change fast enough. You remember those has-beens, right? Ask the taxi industry what Uber is doing to them. Ask the hotel industry how AirBnB is affecting their business. Examples of disruptive change are too numerous to list. But what is clear is that change is a real player in the information age.

There isn't the luxury of time. We used to say, "Wait until this crisis is over and we'll get back to normal," but that never happens. We have to be "change animals."

—MICHELE MCKENZIE, PRESIDENT AND
CEO, CANADIAN TOURISM COMMISSION

In understanding and accepting this ever-increasing rate of change in the information age, we've got only three responses to the change—resist it, accept it, or create it. Only the last sets you up for success.

WHICH ARE YOU? A CHANGE RESISTOR, CHANGE ACCEPTOR, OR CHANGE CREATOR?

Change Resistors: "I like things just they way they are."
For most of us, resistance is the way to go. We resist change out of fear. Change takes us out of our comfort zone, and we don't like that. It's disruptive. It increases our chances

of failure. It puts us in the spotlight, a spotlight we don't like. It requires trust, trust we don't want to give. It requires that we put ourselves out there and expose ourselves to all of the things that come with being *out there*.

Rather than be uncomfortable and embrace change, what do we do? We punt. We say, "Hell, no! I'm not doing that." The problem with this attitude is that it's silly. Change is inevitable. Resisting change puts you at odds with progress. It keeps you from participating in growth.

Resistors are liabilities. They impede success. There is no room for resistors in the information age. No one has the time or inclination to convince you to change. There's no time to coddle, persuade, or cajole.

During the industrial age, change resistors were prized for their stability and predictability, but today the information age has no room for laggards. Today's rate of change demands people who will lead the change and respond to it, not just react, at this pace.

If you're a change resistor, you're in
trouble.

Change Acceptors: "We wait and see what's happening."
Accepting change is safe. When we accept change, we aren't opposed to it. We acknowledge its importance to the big picture, but we lack the strength and the boldness to initiate it. We let others take the lead. We let others take the risk.

We're part of the solution, but only after the risk has been squeezed out. *We value our safety and comfort too much.*

> *Security is mostly a superstition. It does not exist in nature, nor do the children of men as a whole experience it. Avoiding danger is no safer in the long run than outright exposure. Life is either a daring adventure, or nothing.*
>
> —Helen Keller

As change acceptors we offer our support and participation in a metered fashion. We look to see how the change is progressing. We measure its validity by what others are saying and thinking. We pay close attention to others' involvement before we move.

Being a change acceptor is better than being a resistor. We aren't barriers, but we can't be counted on to get out front either. The most we do is to see the change coming and prepare for the transition. We support it and those making it. We grease the skids to make it easier for the change creators to work their magic.

We know what it's going to take to make the transition, and we move through it as predictably, smoothly, and effortlessly as we can, making it as nondisruptive as possible. We start planning ahead of time. We build the relationships we need to minimize its impact on us.

If you're a change acceptor, you're playing it too safe.

It's not enough anymore to support change. The information age requires more than your support; it demands people who facilitate change. Organizations can't afford people who sit on the sidelines waiting for others to lead change. They need more out of their investment in you than "wait and see." Change acceptors have their place, but it's never at the front of the pack.

Success has a low ceiling for change acceptors.

Change Creators: "Change creators are today's problem solvers."
The desire to solve problems drives change creators. They see progress in change. They see how things can be better. They initiate change for the purpose of progress. They recognize that there is no progress, no growth, and no innovation without change. And these things are *exactly* what the information age is demanding.

Change creators subjugate risk and fear to progress and growth. They understand that growth is more important than hiding from the risk of failure, the loss of trust, and the fear of the unknown.

Change creators are dedicated to the advancement of their causes and their organizations. They are tightly bound to the success of their efforts. They know that their value rests in their ability to solve problems and grow. Change creators walk with their heads held high, constantly scanning the horizon and looking for opportunities to innovate and improve.

Today's world prizes problem solvers.

The information age is becoming increasingly competitive. Problems are bigger, hairier, and more complex. Solutions are required faster and expected to be more innovative and substantive. Companies are desperate for those who don't wait and are out in front of problems, creating opportunities. Companies want to harness that kind of mind power and responsiveness to the competitive pressures of today's market.

Change creators pull organizations
forward.

- Change creators deliver the most value.
- Change creators are where growth, innovation, and problem solving happen.

- They provide the competitive advantages.
- They create the new innovative products.
- Change creators identify new processes, structures, markets, features, and opportunities—and bring them to life!
- Change creators make us more profitable.
- Change creators keep us from becoming too slow.
- Change creators keep us from becoming bureaucratic.
- Change creators keep driving us forward.
- Change creators create!
- Success in today's world requires creators, and that's what change agents do!

The World Is Demanding to Be Pushed—Are You Pushing?

The world is desperate for change creators. The information age is moving at light speed and it needs those who can navigate the accelerating rate of change. Companies, governments, and communities need people who can keep us from falling behind and help us stay ahead of the curve, avoid stagnation, and stay competitive. We need those who can lead us through the inevitable changes we will face.

This age in human history will belong to the nimble and flexible. It will belong to the change creators. Is that you?

CHAPTER 5

HAVE THE BALLS TO
MAKE IT HAPPEN

---

*There is no passion to be found playing
small—in settling for a life that is less than
the one you are capable of living.*

—NELSON MANDELA

JIM KEENAN

You CAN DO every other thing in this book, but if you don't have the balls to take risks—to put yourself out there and play to win and not not-to-lose—you're never going to make it. You will never reach your potential if you're playing small and don't have the balls to take risks, sometimes big risks.

TAKING RISKS IS INHERENT TO SUCCESS

There is no success without risk. That's a fact—one you need to get comfortable with. You have to be willing to push the envelope. You have to be comfortable with being uncomfortable. Taking risks means:

- Doing something you've never done that you don't even know how to do…yet.
- Exposing yourself to the criticism of others.
- Putting your comfort zone on the chopping block and accepting that it's gonna get whacked.
- Opening yourself up to failure, loss, exposure, and ridicule.
- Walking alone, against the status quo.
- Not accepting what you're told.
- Removing the safety net.
- Giving up the comfort of the known and predictable for the unknown and unpredictable.
- Accepting no boundaries.
- Going for it.

52

MEET LAUREN

Lauren was sixteen, a high school dropout and single mom with a newborn baby. She had been ridiculed and bullied during her teenage years. Her family was poor so she lacked trendy clothes. She was plump and lacked the "girlish figure" society so craves. Life wasn't looking good for Lauren.

Lonely, scared, and unskilled, Lauren started working where she could to make ends meet. She started in a local grocery store and later became a barmaid and hated it. It wasn't conducive to seeing her son, Jordan. She took a job as a taxi dispatch clerk in order to spend more time with her son. Although she was now spending more time with

Jordan, it didn't take long to realize that if she didn't do something different, life would be very difficult.

With nothing more than an idea and computer, Lauren decided to start an online business selling cosmetics. She saved what little money she could and built a little inventory. After a short while, orders started coming in. Excited, she decided to start taking pictures of the makeup applied to the face rather than just sharing pictures of the makeup bottles. This kicked her business in the butt and she started receiving hundreds of e-mails a day. Unable to respond to them all, Lauren had an idea that would change everything.

It was a scary idea. It meant she would have to risk being bullied all over again. It meant she risked being ridiculed and made fun of. She had to get out of her comfort zone and put herself out there.

Lauren decided she would create makeup tutorial videos of herself demonstrating how to apply the makeup. Lauren was terrified.

A pudgy, single teenage mother who had been bullied because of her appearance, lack of style, and insecurity was now going to put herself on YouTube applying makeup for the world to see. *Now that's some balls!*

Here was a girl whose teenage years were so tortured that she categorized her high school experience as "five years of hell." She had every excuse not to put herself out there.

Reasons not to take risks are a lot easier to
come by than reasons to take them.

And Lauren had a treasure trove of reasons not to take the risk. It would have been far too easy for Lauren to avoid making those videos. The bullying was bad enough in high school. Imagine millions of bullies from around the world piling it on? It could have been hell all over again. Yet she did it anyway. She had the balls to put herself out there and go for it.

This single decision became the catalyst to Internet fame and business success.

Lauren Luke's makeup tutorial videos have received millions of views. YouTube invited her to be one of its first video partners to get a share of the ad revenue. She launched her own cosmetic line "by Lauren Luke," which is now in 135 Sephora stores around the United States and Canada. She tours the country in a giant pink tour bus to greet huge crowds clamoring to get a glimpse of this Internet celebrity and makeup genius. She has a book: *Looks by Lauren*. She is a writer and makeup expert for *The Guardian*. She even has an avatar in Nintendo DS video game called "Supermodel Makeover, by Lauren Luke."

The single decision to expose herself to the world and risk being bullied, ridiculed, poked fun of, and laughed at changed everything in Lauren Luke's life. Lauren would have been completely justified in not doing makeup tutorials. But she took the risk anyway—as she should have.

SUCCESS IS A CHOICE, AND IT STARTS WITH TAKING CHANCES

If you want to be successful in the information age, you have to have the balls to take some risks. Play outside of what you've known and put some skin in the game. Have the balls to get out of your comfort zone. That's where the magic happens.

It takes balls to put yourself out there, to risk your life savings, to expose yourself to ridicule, to challenge the status quo, to be different, to look silly, to take the path less traveled, to quit your job, to invest in that start-up, to open a bakery, to make a movie, to say, "Ya know what? I'm doing it!" Because if you don't, you will not reach your potential, you will not see the success you want.

WHAT HAVE YOU BEEN AFRAID TO DO? GO DO IT!

Start that online business. Tell your boss the marketing campaign is a piece of shit and that you've designed a better one that will increase leads and drive more revenue. Ask out the guy in Unit 9A you've been staring at for months. Start a blog. Buy that new camera, and start taking pictures and putting them on Flickr. Move to San Diego and start working for a surf shop. Take a cut in pay and move into product development. Introduce the new product that everyone thinks is a bad idea except you.

Unlike the other keys to success in this book, there is no step-by-step approach here. I can't give you a script on how to "go for it." It's simply up to you. You just have to go for it. It's a simple binary decision: "Yes, I will do it," or "No, I won't."

Whatever you do, have the balls to take some risks and go for it. I promise that if you don't, someone else will. Don't get caught waving to the world as it passes you by.

CHAPTER 6

THINK

"*Five percent of the people think;
ten percent of the people think they think;
and the other eighty-five percent would rather
die than think.*"

—THOMAS EDISON

THE WORLD HAS BECOME TOO COMPLEX *NOT* TO THINK

IN 2010, IBM interviewed over 1,500 CEOs worldwide—those men and women charged with thinking for their organizations, thinking about how, where, when, and what they can do to grow their company, and responsible for hundreds of billions of dollars in revenue. Collectively, these CEOs were freaking out that their enterprises weren't ready for the future. A whopping 79 percent said that they see business getting more and more complex and that they don't have the talent and leadership to navigate it.

It'll take a new paradigm and new leadership to navigate the increasing complexities of the information age. This is new leadership that the world's top CEOs don't believe they have and a new paradigm they aren't prepared to address.

LET ME TELL YOU A CHRISTMAS STORY

I was in Wal-Mart. The lines were long, as you'd expect. After about five minutes, I stepped to the cashier as the man ahead of me started to walk away. Before the cashier had time to start ringing me up, the man came back holding up the item he just bought: a package of two ceramic Tabasco™ decorative jugs, one cracked. It was clear that he hadn't noticed this until he was walking away. He couldn't have gotten ten feet before turning back. But when he presented the broken item to the cashier, she was baffled and pointed him to the line for returns. She said there was nothing she could do. He'd just have to return it and get another one.

Here's the problem: the returns line was easily twenty people long, spilling into the main aisle. I can't say for sure, but my guess is that it was a thirty- to forty-five-minute wait at least.

The customer pointed this out to the cashier and reminded her that he had literally just bought it ten seconds before. The cashier looked at him in complete bewilderment. She had absolutely no idea what to do. So, of course, she followed the only thing she could think of (what she was taught); she sent him to returns.

That is ludicrous! Had this cashier been thinking about how to solve this problem and had she kept the customer in mind, she had a number of options. She could have had him go get one that was not cracked and then labeled the broken one as damaged. She could have called over a manager and explained the situation. The cashier had alternatives *if* she chose to think.

Because of her inability or unwillingness to think:

- The customer had a bad experience.
- The returns team had an extra person in an already long line.
- The cashier herself missed an opportunity to demonstrate her added value as an employee.

(I have no idea if the customer said to hell with it and found a manager—which is what I would have done—or went with it and exchanged the product.)

For all intents and purposes, this was a small problem. It doesn't take rocket science to make it right for the customer. But this Wal-Mart employee couldn't do it. She got stuck in her habit of doing, not thinking. It happens all too often.

We're operating on autopilot
and it's killing our dreams and stunting our success.

If people are struggling to solve little problems like this, imagine how hard it is to solve the big hairy problems businesses face every day. It wasn't too long ago that this type of compliance and rule-following was expected and admired. "Follow the rules," they said. And you better have listened.

You see, there was a boss. The boss told you what to do and then the person who could do it best won. That's how it worked. The people who thought for themselves, who had fresh ideas, who thought of ways to do things better were troublemakers, nuisances. Business didn't care for independent thinkers. Businesses were considered finely tuned machines where humans were cogs. Everyone had a job and was expected to do it as told. Some cogs were meant to think; everyone else was meant to do. Thinking came from the top, from a select few.

It's from this environment that comes one of my favorite quotes: "I don't pay you to think." It's my favorite because of its sheer stupidity.

Following instructions, doing what you were told, and not rocking the boat were the keys to success during the industrial age. Coming up with a new process, challenging the current system, or doing anything different were career-limiting moves, if not outright career-enders. Those who did what they were told, and did it well, were the prized employees.

Shit! Thank goodness those days are frickin' over. To think we spent years in college honing our craft only to be told what to do. What a waste!

Nonetheless, too many of us have been conditioned in this environment and are not thinking enough. We've forgotten how! We lost our way in a pre-scripted world where most of our thinking is done for us and very little is expected from us. We've lost our ability to solve big, freaky, scary, hairy problems. And *that's* a problem.

Why? The information age has ushered in a world that is far more complex than it has ever been. Technology, availability of information, massive amounts of data, the Internet, globalization, government regulation, the speed of change, and more have all made doing business increasingly complex.

The World Has Changed

It demands more than doers—it demands thinkers. If you're not prepared to be a world-class thinker, success will elude you. To have success in today's world requires thinking—independent thinking. You have to be able to see problems coming and solve problems for yourself and for others. You have to identify opportunities for change. You have to create solutions that move you and the organization forward. You have to get comfortable working with new and untested data.

Our CEO friends shared their thoughts on what successful leaders of the future would do. Here's what they said:

- invite disruptive innovation
- invite others to drop outdated approaches and take balanced risks
- consider previously unheard-of ways to drastically change the enterprise for the better
- be comfortable with ambiguity
- be brave enough to make decisions that alter the status quo
- experiment and invent new business models based on entirely different assumptions

Take a good long look at each of those requirements. What is the underlying need of each of them? That's right…they require you to *think*. They cannot be accomplished, in any way, without taxing your synapses.

IN TODAY'S WORLD, YOU'RE NOT PAID TO *DO*, YOU'RE PAID TO *THINK*

Employers are paying for your ideas, your thoughts, and your ability to solve problems creatively. They need new perspectives. They want to break the status quo. They want people who are going to solve the complexities and difficult challenges that are increasingly stunting business growth today.

Complexity requires collaboration. Collaboration is just thinking together. The more complex something is, the more people are required to solve the problem. Corporations and society in general are beginning to understand this, and it is driving up the value of thinking.

In the 1980s, corporations retained information, and you had to go ask for it. It was a typical do-what-I-say environment with entrenched gatekeepers. There was no Internet. (Try not to hyperventilate, millennials. I know it's crazy, but it's true.)

LEADERSHIP STYLES VS. INFORMATION

1980s	RETAIN INFORMATION, PEOPLE NEED TO COME AND ASK
1990s	CONTROL, DISTRIBUTE EVENLY AND ENSURE IT IS NOT WIDELY ACCESSIBLE
2000s	COMMUNICATE THE INFORMATION AND TRANSLATE IT ACCORDING TO THE AUDIENCE
2010s	SHARE THE INFORMATION AND GUIDE THE AUDIENCE TO FIND IT AND UNDERSTAND IT
Future	ENCOURAGE VALUABLE INFORMATION CREATION AND LEVERAGE IT

Source: Early Strategies Consulting

Information was expensive, and the top brass held on to it. There was little interest in what you thought. Since you weren't paid to think, you didn't need the information. In the 1990s, they let up a bit but still had heavy control on information. Information was distributed to a select few, those who were paid to think. In the early 2000s, leadership started to get hip to the value of information. (Notice the timing here? Internet anyone?) They began moving away from command-and-control management and started to engage workforces from the bottom up and top down. They began to communicate, translate, and share information.

THINKING BECAME EVERYONE'S JOB

Today companies are fully dedicated to becoming thinking organizations, encouraging employees to create information. It's no longer a top-down exercise. Companies expect employees to bring and leverage new information, ideas, and insights to drive innovation, change, and growth. The world has become too complex to win if thinking is reserved for the select few who sit at the top of the organizational chart.

The importance of critical thinking—the ability to analyze and assess, ask essential questions, identify strengths and weaknesses, develop strategies, filter for bias, see trends, follow logic, and more—has been elevated to new heights. Being a critical thinker means you:

- expand upon the information you take in
- when faced with problems or new situations, don't default to a single solution or what you were told
- look at the bigger picture, consider the context, look for contradictions, and embrace the broader vision or goal
- if you have time, research alternatives
- don't accept everything as status quo (sometimes there are better solutions)
- leverage information to anticipate future problems, opportunities, risks, solutions, and so on.

Success in today's world comes to those who can
do more than *do*.
It comes to those who can *think*.

Putting your head down and doing what you've always done will no longer yield the benefit it once did. There are few pats on the back for being a "yes man" in today's world. Waiting to be told what to do isn't going to endear you to anyone any longer.

If you want to crush it in the information age, you have to be a thinker. Train your mind to solve easy, difficult, and big hairy problems. Ask yourself:

- What can I do to make this situation better?
- What could we do differently here to improve this product, process, or approach?
- How can I add value to this situation, job, company, goal, or team?

That's what companies want in today's workplace, and those who can add value by outthinking everyone else will be the winners.

CHAPTER 7

LEARN HOW TO SELL

Nothing happens until something gets
sold.

THAT'S RIGHT. *NOTHING.*

You've got the hots for that chick or dude in your office? Great, but ain't nothing going to happen until you get him or her to pay attention to you and agree to go out with you. If you don't think that's selling, then this chapter is going to be long and painful.

You have this great idea for a new product at your company? Good for you, but it ain't goin' nowhere if you can't convince management that it's worth it.

You desperately want a job with the hot new start-up that called you last week? Good for you—so does everyone else. You ain't gonna get it if you can't sell yourself.

You're thinking about starting a new business. Awesome! But good luck if you can't sell because you won't get funding, you won't get new customers, and you won't get good employees.

Selling is the key to everything in society. If you can't sell, you're screwed. It's that simple.

If you're that person who says they hate sales and can't sell, you're putting a nail in your own coffin. As much disdain you may have for sales, it does not change the fact that selling is at the core of *every* transaction in society.

For you sales-haters and those who feel they can't sell and so it's not worth it, I'm gonna break it down for you.

If you can't sell, you have no influence.
If you have no influence, you aren't directing your life.
It's directing you.

Sales Is Just Another Word for Influencing Change

It's really that simple. Sales is the catalyst for change influenced by someone or something else. Sales is change, and by now, you are a change-maker, right? You strive for change that's tilted toward your benefit, your needs, your wants, your desires. Then you've got to learn how to sell.

What do the most successful people in the world, past and present, have in abundance that average people don't? Influence. Successful people have an uncanny knack for influencing the masses. They have the ability to get their ideas adopted no matter how big or small they are.

I have a dream that my four little children will one day live in a nation where they will not be judged by the color of their skin, but by the content of their character.

—REVEREND DR. MARTIN LUTHER KING, JR., AUGUST 28, 1963

Martin Luther King sold us all on the necessity that we recognize the content of one another's character and not skin color. What's more, he sold millions of black Americans—angry, frustrated, and disenfranchised black Americans—on peaceful civil disobedience, not violence, as the route to equality. That is one giant sales job, one of the best ever.

In order to drive the change we want in our lives, we must influence the people and the environments around us. We have to be able to get people to follow us, embrace our ideas, buy into our vision, back our approach, be in our corner, and give us money. The only way to do that is through influence. And that's selling.

HERE'S THE GOOD NEWS: ANYONE CAN LEARN TO SELL

There is no special sauce. It's not something you're born with. Unlike conventional wisdom, you don't have to be charismatic or gregarious. You simply have to give a shit.

Yup, selling is that simple.

To be a killer salesperson, you simply have to give a shit about the people and environment in which you're selling. If you care enough about the people you are trying to "sell" to and are keenly focused on what it is they need and how you can improve their world, selling becomes easy.

Let me say that again: *focus on improving their world*. True selling isn't about misrepresenting, lying, manipulating, overpromising, or being deceptive. That's being a con man. That's being a scumbag. We've all seen and experienced these douche bags. They aren't salespeople—they're charlatans. They take advantage of people's ignorance and naïveté.

True selling means understanding the needs, goals, and problems of your prospects, friends, family, bosses, collaborators, and everybody else within your sphere of influence. True selling involves bringing positive change to the current environment. It's about helping people see an alternative, providing a vision of what the future could be versus the current scenario.

To be good at sales, you need these three related skills: *problem finding*, *problem solving*, and *storytelling*. Nail these and you will have the foundation for being a killer salesperson.

FIRST, FIND THE PROBLEM

The reason so many think "selling" is a four-letter word is because they see it as trying to get people to buy shit they don't need. That couldn't be any further from the truth. Selling is just the opposite—it's about helping people solve a problem.

If you want to be a good salesperson, you need to get good at finding problems. If there is no problem, there is no sale. The best salespeople are badasses at finding problems. They ask a million questions. They become experts in their industry or area of influence. They understand human nature and what makes people tick. Great salespeople don't push product; they spend their time identifying problems they can solve. They know that if they can solve a problem, the sale is half done.

Finding problems is all about being inquisitive, asking questions, and assessing situations. Get to the root of the situation and ask:

- What's not working?
- What could be different?
- What could improve this situation?

- What could make this person, this company, this group, or this family's life better?

After critically analyzing your surroundings and the goals and objectives of others, you become aware of where you can help. You get in tune with the power of change and how situations can be transformed. Once you have this, you are in the driver's seat.

Once you know how to make someone's world better, they want to listen to you. They want to learn about your idea, product, service, approach, or solution. They are ready to be influenced.

Learning how to sell starts with being a problem finder. When we find problems, that's when everything starts to change.

Don't believe me? Think about the job interview. Bet you didn't see that coming, did you? Yet it's one of the most common sales everyone makes multiple times in their lives. The job interview is unequivocally a sales call.

Typically, we go in prepared to demonstrate our skills and knowledge. We study the company to show we did our homework. We prepare ourselves to show that we have the requisite experience and knowledge to be hired. We articulate our strengths. We highlight our accomplishments. We spend the entire interview answering why we are the perfect candidate.

Unfortunately, this approach is completely wrong and often hurts us. Why? Because when we interview like this, we're not selling, we're telling. Telling is not selling.

Think about the last interview you had. What were the three biggest problems the company was looking to solve with a new hire? Can you accurately describe what the hiring manager was struggling with and the specific problem he or she was trying to solve? If you're like most, you have no idea. In that case, you weren't selling, only telling. And telling ain't selling.

We do this because we don't know better. We've never learned to uncover problems. We've never been taught to identify the problems that hiring managers are looking to solve by hiring someone new.

In today's world, however, the best candidates waste little time "telling" employers about how great they are. Instead, they spend the interview asking questions to understand the hiring manager's issues. Then they engage in a conversation about how their skills, expertise, knowledge, and capabilities can solve those pressing problems. These people recognize that the interview is a sales call. And you can bet that they get the job offer.

Get good at finding folks' problems
and you're gonna see the world in a completely different way.
You'll be on your way to being a badass salesperson.

SECOND, SOLVE THE PROBLEM

Once you've identified the problem, you have to be able to solve it. Solving problems moves people from their current undesirable state to a better one. To be a killer salesperson, you have to understand what a good solution looks like. If you don't have a good solution, if you can't solve the problem, don't even try.

The solution can be anything. The solution can be you as a candidate for a new job. The solution can be your idea for a new strategic direction, a third-party product, or a suggested action. It can be a suggestion to stop doing something or to start doing something else. The range of solutions is infinite.

The key is less about what the solution is and more about understanding if it will be able to solve the problem and how well. The better your solution can solve the problem, the better chance you have of selling it.

The best salespeople in the world are the best problem solvers. They create, identify, and leverage better solutions. They know how solutions solve problems and are excellent at articulating how that solution will affect change.

To get good at selling, get good at solving problems.

Learn to look to make change. Learn to be a problem solver in all aspects of your life. Learn what it will take to solve the problems in your marriage. What will it take to improve your relationship with your spouse? Learn to solve the problems with your children. What solution can you come up with to get your teenage daughter to put the phone down and spend more time with you? Learn what it will take to bring your team to the next level. What solution can you devise to get your team to spend more time building the pipeline? Learn to solve the problems you have with your boss. What solution do you have to help her feel comfortable investing in the new idea you have to grow sales? All of the challenges and opportunities in life from work to home require that we learn to create solutions.

Creating solutions is the creative part in selling. It's what we do with all the data we've been able to acquire. The key to finding the problem involves asking questions, and all those questions give us insights and direction, which we can then leverage to create a solution. Better solutions create better outcomes, better outcomes equal greater value, and everyone loves greater value. The better we get at creating solutions, the more in demand we become.

Find the problem, solve the problem, and then tell a damn good story.

FINALLY, TELL THE STORY

This is where it all gels—the sales story. Once you've identified the problem and the solution, it's all about delivery. How you tell the story, how you frame the story, is how you win.

Telling the story well means you have the ability to deliver your solution in a way that captures the emotional and logical parts of your audience. Another way of looking at this combination is tension and desire* (from Pitch Anything, Oren Klaf.)

Desire is our emotional response; tension is our logical response. "Will it work?" "I want it, but will it solve my problems?" "It sounds good, but will it get me what I'm looking for?" Creating this tension between emotion and logic captures your audience and gets them engaged in what you are selling.

Wanna get good at creating tension? Wanna get good at tapping into emotion? Start with knowing your audience. Get close to them. Understand who they are.

Remember, selling isn't about you—it's about them.

Once you're clear on who you are selling to, start with intrigue. Frame your story in a way that intrigues them. Offer them something they didn't know already. Provide data or insight they were unaware of. When you do this, your audience sticks around because they want the answer. They're gonna listen. People hate not having the answer.

Now that you have them hanging on your every word, it's time to deliver your pitch—the sale. This is where you get to share all the reasons why your solution is valuable and a benefit to them.

This is the most important part of knowing how to sell. The pitch, the sale, the story must focus on the benefits to the person you're selling to. I know you want your kid to eat his broccoli, but your goal is to get him to see why he needs to eat his broccoli. I know your company needs to adopt a new process or your job becomes harder, but it's your goal to get them to recognize that productivity and profits will decrease if they don't adopt the new process.

What matters is how the story emotionally and intellectually affects your audience. Get good at focusing keenly on what the audience needs, why they will benefit from your idea, and what will happen if they don't. That's what makes the story matter.

SALES IS ABOUT GIVING VALUE

In the end, selling is the ability to bring value to the people around you. Value is at the core of a healthy economy and exchange. The greater the value, the greater the demand.

Unfortunately, if value can't be articulated, it might as well not exist. That's why selling is so important. Selling is the ability to convey value through influence and engagement. If you want to grow your career, if you want to achieve greater levels of success, if you want better relationships, and if you want more time, money, and so on, you have to create value.

Life is an ongoing value equation. Every decision we make is rooted in a value decision. We ask ourselves, "Does doing this versus that give me the value I'm looking for?" Good salespeople thrive at this constant evaluation. They challenge, support, inform, and educate people who are at this decision intersection in order to help them make the best decision possible. Those who give this guidance best are more successful.

Influence + Engagement + Knowledge + Value = Sales

Write it down, highlight it, learn it, embrace it, and solve for it.
It's the best and most fulfilling equation you'll ever need to know.

CHAPTER 8

SCREW YOUR DEGREE

Beware. Your degree is not a proxy for your ability to do any job. The world only cares about—and pays off on—what you can do with what you know (and it doesn't care how you learned it).

—THOMAS FRIEDMAN, WRITING IN THE *NEW YORK TIMES* ABOUT THE HIRING CONSIDERATIONS OF GOOGLE'S SENIOR VICE PRESIDENT OF PEOPLE OPERATIONS, LASZLO BOCK

LOL! I CAN'T help but start laughing as I write this. I know what you're thinking. You're thinking I'm an idiot and that suggesting we screw our degrees is stupid.

I can see the disdain on your face now. I can imagine the anxiety, irritation, and maybe even anger bubbling up inside you. I bet you're thinking, "I spent years busting my hump to get my degree. And I'll be damned if this dumbass is gonna tell me it's worth shit."

OK, let me ease your mind a bit. You're not the first person to call me a dumbass and...I'm not saying your education is worth shit. I'm saying that the piece of paper, your diploma, is—the one we've coveted for centuries, the one hanging on the wall in your office that certifies you've completed the requisite courses and programs. *That* is a piece of shit. It does little to highlight your true value and what you are capable of doing.

Degrees Were Once a Differentiator

During the industrial age, when information was sparse and hoarded, acquiring knowledge meant access to places like universities. Degrees meant something back then— before the Internet, before equal access, and before the ubiquity of student loans. It was common to assume that those with degrees had more knowledge, understanding, and exposure than those without. It was far more difficult for those who chose not to go to school to acquire the same knowledge as those who did. Degrees suggested more than accomplishment; they validated exposure to information and knowledge that others couldn't access.

Access (to education) has never ensured absorption
or retention—just exposure.
Lots of idiots secured degrees.

Today, information is ubiquitous. Universities publish their courses free on the Internet for anyone who wants to take them. You don't get a grade, but if you want to learn what those who've been admitted to MIT or Harvard are learning, you just get online and dig into edX.

EdX is a partnership between MIT and Harvard, and hosts free online courses from both. The same information available to paying students is there for the rest of us without paying $75,000 a year for the prestige of in-person attendance. If you don't like edX, try Coursera. Coursera gives you access to the courses of some of the world's best universities.

Information is everywhere now. It's no longer an issue of access. Therefore, a degree that certifies you've had access is far less valuable than it used to be. We've all got access.

WHAT'S MORE IMPORTANT THAN YOUR DEGREE TO BE SUCCESSFUL TODAY?

The acquisition of knowledge *and* what you are capable of doing with it. It's not enough to have the degree that says you know something—you actually have to know it plus what to do with it. You've got to have a plethora of knowledge and know how to deliver on that knowledge.

You know that really big company filled with really frickin' smart people with a market cap of $380 *billion*? Google. Well, they figured some shit out.

GPAs are worthless as a criteria for hiring,
and test scores are worthless…
we found that they don't predict anything.

—Laszlo Bock, Google's Senior Vice
President of People Operations

Google's research tells us that college degrees are not predictive and that using them to hire is a waste of time. Some teams at Google are staffed as high as 14 percent with non-college grads. That doesn't seem to be hurting them in the marketplace, huh?

What Does Google Prize?

Google doesn't value IQ so much as it does learning ability, the ability to process on the fly. This is the ability to do something with the information you have or do something with the information you pull together from the environment you're in—you know, "thinking." Do you remember that chapter? Are you seeing the theme here?

In addition, Google prizes *emergent leadership*. When faced with a problem as a member of a team, do you step in and lead when the time is right? And just as critically, do you step back and stop leading and let someone else when the time is right for that? Do you know when the time is right?

Next, Google values *humility and ownership*. Google wants to know you have the ownership to step in and try to solve a problem and also to step back and embrace the ideas of others. What Google is looking for are people who can solve problems together as a team. There is no degree for that.

If you're considering school to get that piece of paper, think again. If you're running around showcasing your degree from that prestigious university, think again.

To be successful in the information age, a degree isn't what you need. What you need is knowledge and the cognitive ability to learn new things and solve really crazy difficult problems. The ability to *think* is exactly what Google wants from its employees, and they don't care where you get it or how you learn to do it. They just want it.

It's Time to Embrace Learning for Learning's Sake

So what to do?

- Shift your focus from acquiring a degree to acquiring useful knowledge.

- Develop your thinking and problem solving skills.
- Learn how your mind works. Start by asking yourself how you address difficult problems. How do you leverage the information you have? How do you get more of it?
- Hone your soft skills like leading, humility, creativity, accountability, ownership, collaboration, adaptability, and more.
- Bring a passion for the content you need to submerge yourself in.

The days of cramming to retain just enough to get an A, only to forget everything a semester later, are coming to an end. If you want to excel in this new world, you have to learn to be a sponge. Learn to solve problems on the fly. Learn to work well with others. Take ownership, bring value, and stop focusing on a piece a paper that is quickly becoming a depreciating asset.

WHEN IT COMES TO HIGHER EDUCATION, THE INFORMATION AGE IS CHANGING THE GAME

Degrees used to be a great investment. But the value of the "degree" is declining rapidly, starting with the cost of getting a degree, which is going through the roof. The average college graduate enters the workforce with $30,000 of debt. For what? What do they get for this debt? If you were to ask a thousand college graduates what their degree is worth, I suspect that most will tell you nothing.

Peter Thiel, the Facebook investor, argues that higher education is a bubble and has set up a fellowship that invests in gifted kids who don't want to go to college but would rather become entrepreneurs. Tech investor and *Tech Crunch* columnist James Altucher says college isn't worth the rising tuition. He says, "Not only is college a scam, but the presidents know it. That's why they keep raising tuition." You already know what Laszlo Bock and Google think.

They have all recognized that the days of degrees are quickly yielding to something more worthwhile—the ability to solve problems, work together, and deliver results.

WITH ALL THIS SAID, I'M NOT SUGGESTING YOU *NOT* GO TO COLLEGE

What I'm saying is, don't go just for that piece of paper. Focus higher. Go to acquire and absorb the information that's going to make you more valuable and enhance your ability to deliver. Go to grow *brand you*.

If you happen to get a degree along the way, well then, good for you! Your office wall will thank you.

CHAPTER 9

Experience versus Expertise

You MIGHT WANT to sit down for this, particularly if you're older than thirty-five. You're not going to like what I've got to say. It's completely contrary to what we've been told our entire lives. *Your experience no longer matters.*

Yeah, I said it. Suck it up. Like a college degree, experience doesn't get you what it once did.

Few could care less how *long* you've been doing something. They care more about how well you *know* something. Your expertise...that's what people are paying for in the information age. Experience means nothing without it. Experience isn't what we've always thought it was.

CNBC's *The Profit*

The awning was dilapidated. Once a bright and gleaming source of pride, it was now an ominous sign of a quickly failing business. Old, faded, smudged, and outdated, the awning and the business over which it hung were in trouble.

Founded all the way back in 1977, the New York fixture Car Cash was hemorrhaging cash. The owners, two brothers who had inherited the business from their father, were struggling to keep the doors open. Working on razor-thin, unsustainable margins, the Barron brothers were just weeks away from closing their doors, when Marcus Lemonis walked through their door.

Marcus Lemonis is the CEO of Camping World and Sam Good Enterprises. He's also the charismatic and no-nonsense entrepreneur in the new hit reality television series *The Profit*.

In *The Profit*, Lemonis goes around the country looking for depressed and in-trouble businesses, and then he puts in his own money to turn them around. In the Car Cash episode, Lemonis saw an opportunity and not only turned the company around but also turned it into a nationally licensed franchising company. The Barron brothers now have two locations, and Lemonis is licensing the concept nationwide with stores opening everywhere. Lemonis has turned around everything from a frozen yogurt company to a gym, a meat-packing company to an eco-friendly cleaning products company, all in plain view of the world.

The Profit gives us more than just a study of a smart entrepreneur with a knack for turning around companies; it highlights what really matters to success—expertise, not experience. Every entrepreneur on the show had more "experience" in their particular field than Lemonis. Each and every one of the company owners had worked longer in their respective field. Some even had more business experience than Lemonis. Yet Lemonis, with little to no experience in gyms, cleaning products, or frozen yogurt, turned them around. How?

He has more expertise, tremendous business expertise. It's not experience that Lemonis is leveraging when he's working his magic on the show; it's the depth of his business expertise. Lemonis knows business. He understands how to make a profit. He knows what it takes to produce a packaged good. He knows how to manage people, and he knows how to build processes that work. It's this *expertise* that has made Lemonis successful. Lemonis is only forty-three years old. There are lots of people out there with more business experience, just not as many with his expertise.

To be successful in the information age, you have got to stock up on expertise
and stop measuring experience.

EXPERIENCE DOESN'T MATTER–EXPERTISE DOES

Experience is simply the amount of time you've been doing something, your hours of participation in a particular task. It says nothing about what you actually know about that something.

Experience assumes a level of absorption. It assumes you gained expertise through time spent. But that's a *bad* assumption. Just because someone has been doing something for a long time doesn't mean they are experts. Experience only correlates to experience. Experience is not a synonym for expertise!

Some people have 10 plus years experience yet only 2 years of expertise, while others have just 2 years of experience, and 10 years of expertise. The key is to have your expertise outpace your experience.

Experience isn't hard to acquire. It's based in staying power. If someone can figure out how to do their job just well enough in order to hang around just long enough and keep from getting fired, they can gain extensive experience. That does *not* mean they are building much expertise. It doesn't mean they are acquiring more knowledge. It doesn't mean they've become an expert. It just means they've hung around long enough.

Does expertise come from experience? Yes! But does experience create expertise? Not necessarily.

The false assumption that experience equals expertise has been prevalent in the workplace for years. Finally, in the information economy, folks are getting hip to it and starting to look for expertise.

EXPERTS DELIVER RESULTS AND VALUE

Expertise is the actual amount of knowledge, understanding, precision, effectiveness, accomplishment, and delivery that someone can provide in their role. It's not based on time spent. Experts deliver at higher and higher levels because they have the skills and methodologies to successfully execute and get stuff done.

Experience is empty; expertise is deep.

Experience is nothing more than hours on hours, time stacked on time, time card upon time card, punch clock over punch clock. Experience is empty.

It's expertise that brings experience to life. When two people have the same "experience," their expertise differentiates them. Expertise is how well we've grasped the job at hand so that we can deliver. Those with greater expertise have a much better understanding of the nuances, intricacies, complexities, and approaches to the task at hand.

People with greater expertise play at a
deeper level.
Their expertise allows them to influence and shape
their job, their organization,
and even their industry.

EXPERTISE GOES WAY BEYOND PROFICIENCY AND IS A FORCE MULTIPLIER

Those with experience alone are shaped by their job. The job moves them; they don't move the job. The job dictates what to do and how to do it. Experience by itself causes us to react to our surroundings. We're familiar, we know what's coming, we know what to expect, and so we learn to react better. We become proficient at working within the system.

On the other hand, expertise positions us to direct our working environment. It gives us the power to craft and shape our surroundings to fit our needs. And where there is expertise, innovation isn't far behind. Trends are readily identified. Anomalies are made visible. Opportunities are created. Efficiencies are gained with increases in productivity. More is done with less. Waste is eliminated. Success is highly probable.

BECOME THE EXPERT

Success in today's world means becoming an expert. It doesn't mean being the guy or gal who's been there longer or has done it more. It means being the person who knows more, understands more, and has the expertise to drive the job, not be driven by it. Getting expertise requires a commitment to being the best.

It starts with learning. You have to be willing and want to learn. Dig in. Ask how, when, why, and what happens. Go deeper than everyone else. You have to know more than everyone else about your job *and* everything around it.

Here's how:

1. *Read prodigiously.*
   If you're not reading at least a book a month about your industry, your job, your environment, and the skills required to do what you do, you're not becoming an expert. If you're not reading two or three blog posts a day, you're not learning enough. If you can't make the commitment to read and grow every day, then stop now and accept your current status. The Internet is an expert in everything and is just waiting to make you one, too.

There is no growth without reading, period.

Embed yourself in your job/space/industry *and* its adjacent worlds. Read everything you can about your field and related fields and disciplines. For example, if you're a minister, don't just read the Bible. Read the Koran, the Torah, and every other religious book you can. Look to understand the similarities and differences in each the world's religions. Determine how they have influenced one another and how they have affected their respective times. Ministers with expertise over experience know more than just their tiny world of the divinity.

Here are some other examples:

- If you're in supply chain, read everything you can about supply chain management, inventory, distribution, shipping, logistics, inventory accounting, warehousing, and so on.
- If you're in sales, read about sales leadership, sales processes, selling principles, relationship building, marketing, business, account management, pipeline management, deal strategy, overcoming objections, and sales psychology.
- Or make your own list here.
- I'm in _____. I look forward to reading about and developing expertise in _____, _____, _____,
- _____, _____, and _____.

Never stop expanding your acquisition of knowledge, ever.

2. *Ask questions: Why? What if?*

    Be curious. Don't accept what you've been told. Challenge conventional wisdom. When we challenge the status quo, it's like taking apart a car. It forces us to figure out how all the parts work together, how each component affects every other component. It validates our assumptions, gives us new insights, and spawns creativity.

    Experts move things around. They push, prod, evaluate, and explore how things work. All that digging increases their knowledge, problem solving, and critical thinking.

3. *Look for improvements and add your mark.*

    Experts are not passive in their roles. They get engaged, and so should you. Since experts don't accept the "way we've always done things around here," they are always looking to improve their craft. They look to shorten production, accelerate growth, increase close rates, reduce costs, improve the processes, and make other enhancements. In short, experts are the change creators we talked about in Chapter 4.

BE A PART OF THE FEW

If you're still not convinced that expertise trumps experience, then don't read any further, as you'll just be wasting time. Go back to logging your hours, but don't look out the window so you don't see those passing you by, winning the promotions, job offers, awards, and acknowledgment that you're not. Their careers are overtaking yours because they are experts.

We've been taught for years that experience is what counts—that's a myth. Experience without expertise invites stagnation and a resistance to change. Today's world has less and less need for experience. It's all far too complex and it's desperate for expertise, leaders, and knowledge holders with fresh ideas and solid input.

The demand for experts is high. Everyone has experience. Few have expertise.

CHAPTER 10

TIME VERSUS RESULTS

WHO WANTS UNLIMITED VACATION?

MATT SITS IN a corner office, a big lush office fitting his stature as the CEO of a company in the software as a service (SaaS) industry. It has its own separate meeting space, like a fancy hotel suite. Unlike most CEO offices, however, his is half glass.

The wall that faces into the building is all glass, completely transparent. Matt literally lives in a glass house... okay, works in a glass office. You get my point. The office offers little in the way of visual privacy.

I can't help but wonder if Matt is conscious of the occasional subconscious nose pick. He should be, because there is no hiding in that office. It's this "hiding" idea, or lack of it, that makes Matt's company so interesting.

Beyond the see-through surroundings and complete transparency, there is another unique element to Matt's environment: the array of "thank you" and "I'm thrilled" notes pinned up behind his desk. He's been collecting these cards from happy employees for years. Matt gushes when you ask him about them.

To Matt, these cards validate the culture he's built meticulously over the years—one that embraces transparency, particularly around getting things done. This is especially evident in the fact that Matt's company measures results, not time.

So what does it mean to "measure results and not time"? There are no time cards, and Matt's employees get unlimited vacation time. Yup, that's right. They don't count vacation days or hours. If you want to take two months of vacation, have at it. Vacation time is unlimited, and employees love it. How does a company offer unlimited vacation to its employees? It does this by focusing on results *not* time.

BACK WHEN TIME WAS VALUED

At the turn of the twentieth century, when the world was moving from an agricultural society to a manufacturing one, the demand for human "time" was front and center. Millions upon millions of rote repetitious jobs were created. There was tremendous demand for unskilled labor. People who could follow directions and do the same thing over and over with little error were in high demand. Thinking was *not* part of the job description.

Output and effectiveness were measured in terms of efficiency. Employees were prized for their ability to execute repeatable actions with as few errors as possible. The way we measured and rewarded these efforts was in time. In a world where thinking was not valued, time was the commodity.

The punch card was born, and for the next 100 to 110 years, we valued time. We traded our time for dollars: hourly fees, hourly rates, dollars per hour, punch in, punch out. You were on the clock. Hours were our measure and were at the core of our barter agreement. Our value was measured in the time we gave the company.

We have been so ingrained to measure our time that we still applaud ourselves with statements like, "I spent all day working on that," without taking into consideration whether we actually accomplished what we set out to accomplish. We glorify busy. We still measure and applaud our success by the time we put into something (the effort) rather than by what we delivered (the output). That's not okay in the information age.

SUCCESS TODAY IS INCREASINGLY MEASURED BY RESULTS

Time has little value in Matt's world. He doesn't want your time. He wants what your time enables—the results. Matt is quick to tell you, "What gets measured, gets managed. You manage time, you get time sheets and bickering. If you manage outcomes, you get results."

Matt will also tell you about a company where he worked where everyone had to count hours, even the executives. Everyone was required to use time sheets, and if you exceeded the number of days off, you were docked pay. Everyone got a set number of sick days and vacation days, and had to use them or lose them. As the end of each year approached, there was a mad rush by employees to use all of their unused sick time, healthy or not, and all of their unused vacation time. This mad rush for "time" left the company barely staffed during what turned out to be their busiest time of year.

Matt says, "People who took time off didn't check in, pitch in, help remotely, and so on. So basically you got completely screwed if you took normal vacations during the year because you were 'on call' over Christmas."

How much do you think got done at this company? Not too damn much.

Companies that count hours suck to work for. People who use hours as a reflection of their value suck to work with.

The best example is attorneys. Attorneys could care less if you avoid jail time, don't have to pay that ten million dollars, or are found guilty. They get paid for their time regardless of outcomes. Therapists are time counters, too.

They have no compensation vested in whether or not they save your marriage or if they help you get past your fear of flying. They get paid every time you walk into their office and lay your ass on their couch. They put value on their time regardless of the outcome and at the expense of their customers and clients—you!

If you're still measuring your value in time, how *hard* you work or how many hours you put in, you're headed in the wrong direction. Time is a dying commodity, and companies like Matt's are helping bury time measurement. They are winning because of it.

FEWER AND FEWER COMPANIES CARE HOW HARD YOU WORK, AND NEITHER SHOULD YOU

Most companies these days only care whether or not you get the job done and whether you get it done well. Focusing on the number of hours you put into your work isn't how you become successful. Rather in the information age, your success will be determined by your ability to deliver real, tangible results.

It's not about showing up. Butts in seats provide no value. Providing value these days requires a different perspective and a different measurement. It requires a clear understanding of what you are good at delivering. It requires that you know what your customer wants, what your boss wants, what your company wants, and then give it to them. If you want to crush it in today's world, you need to be keenly focused on delivering results.

YOU'VE GOT TO ATTACH YOUR VALUE TO DELIVERABLES

Take a look at your resume and *LinkedIn* profile. What do they say? How much white space are you dedicating to time-oriented words like these: *focused on, targeted, employed, lead, managed, responsible for, oversaw, liaison for,* and *supported.* These words are not results-oriented. They are stuck in time.

Restructure your world into one that focuses on delivery and results. Represent your value in terms like: *delivered, created, built, invented, moved, structured, sold, saved, collaborated, authored, achieved,* and *made.*

Measure yourself by your results. Build a list of your accomplishments, the results you made happen, and the results you were instrumental in bringing to life.

The more you get done, the more valuable
you are, regardless of how long it took.

In the information age, no one gives a shit how hard you worked or how much time it took. And neither should you! In today's world, we only want to know one thing—can you get it done?

CHAPTER 11

Don't Be Boring

Boring is camouflage.

Look, I don't know how to say this any other way. Boring people suck, and most people are boring.

Yeah, yeah, I know, not you, right?

The truth is, we're boring. We're raised from early on in life not to stand out, not to make waves, not to make a scene, not to be different, and that is prolly the worst advice we've ever been given. Boring people are never remembered.

Too many of us use it to avoid accountability, owner-ship, exposure, rejection, fear, and failure. Rather than put ourselves out there, we choose to blend in like everyone else. That's a huge problem, because winning and being successful means standing out, being different.

You have a business to grow. Sales numbers to make. Products to market. Newscasts to deliver. Jackets to de-sign. A restaurant to run. Whatever it is you have to do... do you want boring, commonplace, uncreative, unoriginal people helping you do it? No! And neither does anyone else.

Boring people are far too uncomfortable being un-comfortable, so they avoid *change*. They do everything they can to stay in their comfort zone. They don't seek new adventures and different experiences. They avoid the unknown, the unproven, and anything that isn't status quo. They're change resistors or change acceptors at best. They limit their reach because nobody's drawn to boring.

Nobody with reach is boring. You don't build reach if you aren't intriguing to other people. After all, no one wants to be read boring shit, watch boring TV, listen to boring speakers, talk to boring people, or hang out at bor-ing shows, boring bars, or boring movies. Get it?

ENGAGEMENT IS THE ANTITHESIS OF BORING

Engaging people stimulate our senses and capture our imaginations. They lure us in with their knowledge, their positive attitude, their experiences, and their unique views and perspectives. They earn our attention with their creativity, unconventional approaches, style, passion, energy, and all the ways they are different. That's what not being boring is all about—being different!

Being different allows people to see our value. It demands we bring something unique to the table, something different in terms of more, faster, easier, and so on. Different, interesting, and unique are at the core of value. It's hard to be the same, uninteresting and common, and still add value.

Not being boring means shedding your sense of fear. It means being comfortable standing out, failing, and being seen. Not being boring means putting yourself out there. It means doing things differently than you were taught.

Get Comfortable Being Uncomfortable

Did you ever watch Robin Williams perform? Nothing boring about him. Imagine running around the stage like he did, sweating profusely, making sounds, contorting your face and your body, all for a laugh. Robin Williams had no problem standing out. He built his entire career on being different, on being seen for putting himself out there. Robin was completely comfortable being uncomfortable.

Get out of your comfort zone. Push your limits of familiarity, and challenge your notion of the world. Expand your world. It's not enough to play in your world; you have to see it and understand it from different perspectives.

I can excuse everything but boredom.
Boring people don't have to stay that way.

—HEDY LAMARR, ACTRESS

When we're not boring, we:

- **Surprise people**. People love the unexpected. Stop being so predictable. Look for ways to do the things that no one is expecting. Surprise the people in your life as often as you can. The best way to surprise people is to learn about them. Become familiar with how they think. What do they expect? How do they move through their lives? What do they enjoy but not do? What are they expecting from day to day? What are they *not* getting that they want? How can you provide more value to their day, week, month, and year that would make them happy or change their lives? What about your customers, clients, even complete strangers? Find ways to surprise them all.
- **Try new things.** This one is hard for people. It's so easy to get caught up in our routines. Stop it. Make

a commitment to do new things on a regular basis. When we try new things, it expands our worldview. It expands our perspective, and that expanded perspective makes us intriguing. The more you know about a lot of things, the more you can offer. People love learning from others. We are particularly drawn to people with a wealth of knowledge. We love sitting next the woman on the plane who has climbed Mt. Everest or the kid who has met the president or the guy who has been to every continent. We gobble up blogs about parenting written by the stay-at-home mother who chronicles all her mistakes and offers fixes. We're intrigued by the people who know things we don't. Be one of those people. Draw people to you through experiences.

- **Are change creators.** Change keeps us on our toes. It keeps us from becoming complacent and dulled. Change forces us to take notice, to be aware and engaged. The constancy of change keeps us focused and alert as we are looking for what's next, what's coming. Be the go-to person for innovative ideas and new approaches, the one who breaks the monotony. Society gravitates to change agents. We evolve from their energy and ideas.

- **Push ourselves to be great.** What are you great at? Are you good at one thing or multiple things? Are you the *best*, the top 5 percent, at anything? How about two things? You need to be. When we get good at things, we become experts. And it does not matter what we're experts at—we are all the less boring and more intriguing for it. Too many of us move through life doing just enough to get by so we can watch football on Sunday, take the family on vacation once a year, drive a decent car, and live in a decent house. We don't get great at anything.

Most of us aren't *great* at anything.
Most of us are average.
We live in the "dabbler" zone.

We dabble because the return on our effort is higher. That is, we get more out of it than we put in. However, once we peak as a dabbler, we start becoming hobbyists and it takes more work to get better. Most people quit rather than put in the extra effort to get fewer and smaller returns. However, it's when we get *great* at something that we stick out, because we can do something most people can't.

For instance, I'm certified by the Professional Ski Instructor Association as a Level 2 Ski Instructor. I ski better than 99 percent of the people in the world. When I go skiing, people watch and ask for tips. They want to ski with me. I know something they don't, and they want some of it.

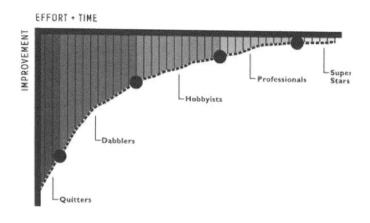

Don't Be Complacent—Get Over That Peak!

When we try something new, we learn it pretty quickly. It doesn't take much to get better. Put in a few hours on the ski slope, and you can be skiing down a bunny hill. Put in a few days, and you can be skiing greens. Put in a week, and you could be skiing blues. In the beginning, the gains for our efforts are favorable—a little bit of effort for reasonable gain. The more effort we put in, the greater the gain or return for that effort.

But as we get better, something evil happens. The return on effort tips. There's a point—called the *peak of positive return*—past which the amount of effort we put in yields very minimal gains. The peak of positive return is where the effort to learn something becomes greater than the benefit we get from the lesson we're learning. We receive a smaller ROI for our time. Therefore, we have to put in more time for fewer improvements. It's tough, but it's how growth works.

This is most poignant with professional athletes. They can train for thousands of hours every year just to shave a hundredth of a second off their time, hit a baseball fifteen more times out of a thousand, or reduce their golf game by two strokes.

When the return on effort tips out of favor, those who push themselves win. They pass the rest of us. They leave the "dabbler" zone and become experts and even professionals. Everybody wants a piece of them because they chose to put in the time and push themselves when it was no longer easy.

You, too, can have people wanting a piece of you. You've got to push past that peak of positive return. *Push, push, push.* Boring people don't push. That's why they are boring. Become great at something, even a couple of things, and get *good* at several more. Don't settle for being average. Don't be a dabbler.

EVADE BORING BY BECOMING A CONNECTOR

In Malcolm Gladwell's best-selling debut, *The Tipping Point*, he talks about the way ideas and trends spread like viruses. A virus needs a host to help it jump from one group to another.

In the life of viruses, that's the person who flies from London to Japan to San Francisco, bringing the infection to new populations. In the life of ideas and trends, that's the person who has lots of friends in different groups and, through them, spreads trends or ideas.

Most of us spend our time with the same people. We spend most of our time with people like us, who think like us, act like us, and view the world like us. However, there are some people who cross social boundaries. They're friends with those like them and also others who are not so much like them.

For example, consider the CEO who spends her workdays engaged with conservative, high-net-worth executives and her weekends with her best friend, the starving artist she met at a festival. In the winter, she teaches skiing and spends time hanging out with twenty- and thirty-somethings on the slopes. In the summer, she loves acting and does a play once a year, hanging out with hip aspiring actors.

She is a connecter. Her relationships, friendships, and contacts in completely diverse groups allow ideas to spread. When she shares something on the ski slope that she heard at the office, that idea penetrates an entirely new group of people. When she learns something in the art world, she shares it at the office, moving yet another idea or trend into an entirely different population.

In spreading ideas, she increases the likelihood that the idea, trend, meme, or whatever will go viral. That's what makes connectors so valuable. They help make ideas and trends go viral. You need to be a connector. You need to build relationships, and a network with lots of different people, in lots of different walks of life. Expand beyond people who are just like you.

KEEP READING

I know, right? Many people think reading is the most boring activity on the planet and a useless suggestion when I'm preaching about *not* being boring.

But stop and think about it. Reading is the acquisition of knowledge. The more you read, preferably nonfiction, the broader your knowledge base. The more interested you are in all kinds of things, the more interesting you become. Renaissance men and women are the most interesting people in the world.

Have you have ever had a conversation with someone who was a fount of knowledge on every subject? I don't mean know-it-alls who possess benign, trite, shallow information on a number of topics; I'm talking a true renaissance person with whom you could have a deep and meaningful conversation on just about anything for hours. These people are a true pleasure to be around. You already know how they got that way—they read!

THERE'S NOTHING BORING ABOUT OUR WORLD, SO LET IT BE YOUR TEACHER

Get out of town! Get out of the state and the country where you live. Travel forces you to have experiences you would not or could not have by staying put in your own little hamlet.

Travel introduces us to new people and cultures. We gain new insights into how others live, what they think, how they engage with other people, and what they prioritize.

The world is a compilation of all the individual choices of humankind. It's all of our cultures, beliefs, and traditions.

When we travel and commit to meeting others, we can't help but be affected. Every person we meet leaves an imprint on us. With more imprints, we become more intriguing.

So get your ass up and see the world. Like the man said:

You have brains in your head.
You have feet in your shoes.
You can steer yourself
any direction you choose.
You're on your own. And you know what you know.
And YOU are the one who'll decide where to go...

—Dr. Seuss

Be Creative

Don't do things like everyone else. Don't wait for social permission. Make your own path. Be creative with the ways you express yourself, even the way you dress. (Hey, businessmen, throw out those stupid, ugly, boring tasseled dress shoes.)

Offer creative solutions to problems at work. Don't default to what you've always done. Throw away preconceived notions of how it's supposed to be done. Look for ways to do things others haven't thought of. Don't view problems from the lens of why they won't work but rather of solutions that will make them work.

Break the rules. Better yet, pretend there are no rules. Don't allow conventional wisdom tell you how to do it and put you in a box. Too often we let the status quo box us in.

Who gets to tell you what is "right" or "wrong"? *You*, that's who.

There is risk in being creative because it makes us different and draws attention. We're on our own. We won't find approval or validation for our creative ideas before we start. Maybe we never will. We have to put them out there naked and raw, subject to the world's criticism and recrimination. When we're creative, we're exposed. That's what makes it so interesting…and keeps us from being boring.

The enemy of creativity…is fear.
We're all born creative; it takes a little while to become afraid.
A surprising insight: an enemy of fear is creativity.
Acting in a creative way generates action, and action persuades the fear to lighten up.

—SETH GODIN

CHAPTER 12

HAVE FUN. BE HAPPY.

Happiness begets success, not the other
way around.

IN THE MID-1980s, the CEO of the insurance company MetLife had a problem. His company was hiring 5,000 salespeople every year. They were spending $150,000,000 every two years in training costs—that's $30,000 per salesperson. That's a lot of money.

No one was sticking around. Half of the salespeople quit in the first year and four out of five quit within four years. That's serious coin walking out the door.

In an effort to stop the bleeding, he reached out to Dr. Martin Seligman of the University of Pennsylvania. Dr. Seligman had long been a proponent of optimism as a deciding factor for success. He argued that success didn't create happiness, but rather that optimistic people became successful because of their positive outlook.

At the time, MetLife screened new applicants for aptitude—their ability to sell. Seligman added a new test to measure optimism. He posited that those who scored higher in optimism would outperform those who tested well for sales.

His thesis proved true. In the group of new hires, the people who flunked the aptitude test but were identified as "super-optimists" outperformed everyone. In the first year, of all who passed the aptitude exam, the optimists outsold the pessimists by 8 percent. By the second year, the optimists outsold the pessimists by 31 percent.

But what makes this story even more compelling is when we compare those "super-optimists" who couldn't even pass the sales aptitude test to the pessimists who did, and the results were astounding.

The "flunkie" optimists outsold the proficient pessimists by 21 percent in the first year and by a whopping 57 percent in the second.
It was absolutely clear that a positive outlook correlated to selling success.

The story doesn't end here. Seligman has taken his optimism test to salespeople across a multitude of industries and the results hold true. Optimistic salespeople outperform pessimistic salespeople from anywhere between 20 percent and 40 percent.

Since Success Follows Happiness, It's Time to Get Happy!

Being happy, having a positive outlook, learning optimism…whatever you want to call it, having fun matters. Having fun deeply impacts our view of the world. It impacts how we view our jobs, our coworkers, our friends, our opportunities in life, our relationships, our financial situation, the economy, our political system, and more. If you want to be successful, you gotta get your outlook in check.

So before we get any further, I want you to be aware and anchored in your own personal view and definition of fun. Let's get real and ask some questions.

How much fun do you have at work? On a scale of 1 to 10, rate the fun you have at work. Be honest with yourself. You don't have to tell anyone and your boss isn't going to know. But write it down and be true.

- How much fun do you have at home?
- Do you have fun all the time? Or only when you're doing things you love, like fishing, working out, Pilates, yoga, skiing, golfing, shopping, and so on?

- Do you only have fun when you're on vacation?
- Can you even have fun when you're on vacation?
- Is fun something you see as a destination or a state of being?
- Do you see fun as something for the weekends, for a ball game, for vacation, for another time?
- How do you see fun? And more importantly, how much energy do you put into having and being fun?

> If you're not having fun, life sucks and it
> will be apparent in everything you do.

We've just seen in the MetLife story that success is not the key to happiness. That's not how it works. Success is the result of being happy and having fun, not the other way around. So let's stop waiting and get happy.

You've Gotta Have Fun and Create Fun

When it comes to having fun and being happy, there are two approaches. First is the ability to let yourself have fun. This involves being open to fun and seeking out situations that are fun and enjoyable. Surround yourself with people who are fun, exciting, engaging, and optimistic...oh yeah, and people who aren't boring! When we let ourselves have fun, we constantly put ourselves in fun situations. We are aware of and gravitate to fun environments and people. When we're not, we don't. That's a problem. Pessimism and negative outlook affect results and negative results don't drive success.

The other approach is to create your own fun without waiting for others to do it for you. Don't rely on external environments to provide fun. Think about it like this. Some people are like toys that need batteries to have fun. They can't create their own energy. They need to find their fun in external energy. Then there are those people who can generate fun all on their own. They are the fun creators. They have a knack for making fun anytime, anywhere. They are the most successful. They build environments that create fun for themselves and everyone around them.

MAKING HAPPY PLACES AND CREATING POSITIVE ENERGY IS WHAT IT'S ALL ABOUT

By creating fun, we give people an opportunity to be happier, more optimistic, more engaged, better connected, and more inspired to get things done. We're drawn to fun creators so they have a wider reach, which means more opportunities and more influence than the sourpusses.

Don't be the mosquito to the light of fun. Be the light.

Fun creators look at the world a little differently, and that's how they are able to add fun to situations and environments where others can't. Fun creators:

- *Don't take things, or yourself, so seriously.* Don't confuse having fun with not being serious or not getting things done. Fun creators know that sometimes the best way to achieve goals is to have fun along the way. The path to the goal will deviate if fun is the only objective. But if you stay focused on the "goal," humor and having fun aren't weaknesses, they're strengths. Fun creators let themselves be vulnerable and silly. Be willing to put yourself out there. Let others see your fun side. Use more humor. There is no room for rigidity when it comes to creating fun. Lighten up, be silly, let your soft side show, put yourself in vulnerable positions, and enjoy the ride. Let others know it's not always just about business.

- *Create fun events.* Fun creators make the fun times happen. They create fun environments, particularly through events. Taking time out of your day to have fun changes moods, relaxes, energizes, inspires, and connects people. Fun creators see the value in environments where people show up to have fun. Fun events don't have to be huge ordeals. They can be as simple as Pizza Fridays or Taco Tuesdays at the office. They can be happy hours, or rolling a TV into the main office during the World Cup or March Madness. It could be a fifteen-minute event, an hour event, or an all-day event whose objective is to simply have fun. Create experiences for people to break up their day and usher them into a happy place. To fun creators, it's all about creating experiences that create positive outlooks.

- *Learn to give more, share more, and take less.* Fun creators know that it's not all about them. They get that the happier the people around them are, the happier they themselves can be. Giving is a huge part of happiness. Studies have shown that giving makes us feel better and contributes to our happiness. Not only does it make those around you happier, it comes back to you. The more you share and the more you give, the happier everyone will be. According to Adam Grant's book *Give and Take*, giving and sharing not only makes you happier, it increases your reach and influence, and makes you more successful. Ya gotta love something that kills two birds with one stone.

BEING HAPPY AND HAVING FUN IS AWESOME... GO BE AWESOME

This is my favorite key to success that no one is teaching you. It's got the greatest return. It affects you and everyone around you. It's so simple, yet at times it can be unbelievably difficult. There are no courses for it. There is no corporate training. Few people are measuring you on your ability to be happy and make others happy. Yet happiness plays a *huge* role in achieving success.

Start a plan today to create happiness and fun in your life with those around you. If you are only successful in one of the skills in this book, this is the one to crush. If you can't or don't execute on any of the others but crush it here, you will be successful regardless of anything else in your life.

CHAPTER 13

DELIBERATE LEARNING

If you're not willing to learn, no one can help you.
If you're determined to learn, no one can stop you.

—Zig Ziglar

ODDLY ENOUGH, I almost didn't write this chapter. I assumed learning was an inherent and implicit characteristic of any successful person. Indeed, I've mentioned it throughout. But I want to make explicit that *deliberate* learning is at the core of all of the other keys to success.

LEARNING IS A CRITICAL KEY TO SUCCESS... DELIBERATE LEARNING IS LEARNING ON STEROIDS

I'd go so far as to say that without a commitment to learning, to deliberate learning, you're fucked. If you are unable to put yourself in a continual learning mode, you can't be successful. You won't accomplish much of anything. It's just too complex of a world. Things change too fast. Companies want us to do more thinking. They want us to deliver more with less direction. Therefore, if we are unable to be lifetime learners, if we're unable to drive our own learning process, we're gonna stall and then we're just gonna stop.

YOU'RE INCOMPETENT AND WORSE, TOO INCOMPETENT TO KNOW IT

Look, I'm sorry I have to say this, but it is highly likely you aren't very good at what you do. You may feel that you are and in many cases you may have been told that you are, but the data and research suggests that you aren't.

In his seminal research David Dunning, in conjunction with Justin Kruger, uncovered a powerful phenomenon, that most of us overestimate our abilities and capabilities. That is we believe we are better than we really are. Not only do we overestimate our skills, we lack the metacognition or ability to even realize we aren't that good. Dunning puts it like this; the dumb get confident, while the intelligent get doubtful. To compound the matter, the less someone knows about a topic or subject, the more overconfident they are about their abilities. It's not until we acquire more and more knowledge that our self-assessment comes inline with our actual capabilities.

It was David's research that drove me to add this chapter. We aren't as good as we want to believe we are and if we want to be successful in the twenty-first century we have to recognize that a growth mindset—the ability to learn, expand our knowledge and adopt new ideas, skills, methodologies and approaches—is critical. And unfortunately, we're not wired that way. We're wired to think we're better than we are and therefore not grow.

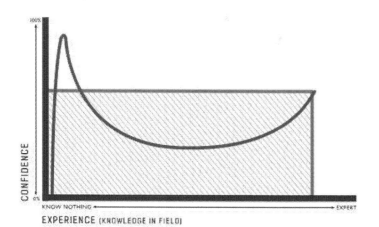

If I still haven't convinced you and you still think you're the shit, research Dunning's paper more. Wikipedia has a decent write-up. Humility is required and so is a commitment to learn more, more often at a more frequent rate, and the first step is to realize you have a lot to learn.

Success is not present in stasis.

We've all heard about the amount of information available to us in the information age. Google's former CEO said we're creating more information every *two* days than was created from the dawn of civilization to 2003. That's some serious information creation. However, the creation of data is meaningless if you aren't able to do anything with it.

Success will pass by those of us who are unwilling or unable to leverage all this data. That's where deliberate learning comes in.

IT DIDN'T USE TO BE THIS WAY...TIMES HAVE CHANGED, HUH?

For most of the twentieth century—that is, the industrial age—learning was an early life endeavor. We were expected to learn in school as children, in college as young adults, and, for a small few, in postgraduate school. But once school was finished, our commitment to learning decreased substantially. Companies didn't demand learning, with the exception of company-sponsored continuing education, or training.

To make matters more challenging, for most of the twentieth century, access to information was difficult. Learning was limited to public libraries, bookstores, mentors, company information banks, or college campuses.

Today, anything we want to learn, know, explore, or understand can be accessed in seconds from our phones, computers, and TVs. The limits to learning have been wiped away. It's just not okay not to know anymore. Companies have less and less patience for those not willing to learn or grow on their own. Successful people are pairing company-taught learning with their own deliberate learning to become knowledge and delivery powerhouses.

If You Want to Be Successful, Commit to Learning on Purpose

Make a conscious deliberate commitment to learning specific measurable things in an effort to become better, more aware, and more knowledgeable in your job and life. Take it to the next level—think of it as strategic learning. Deliberate learners evaluate an objective or goal and ask, "What don't I know? What can I learn to be better at this? What information can I attain that would improve my ability to deliver a better result faster, cheaper, with greater value? What can I learn to help solve this problem?"

Deliberate learners know that success and improvement come from strategically and methodically identifying their knowledge gaps and filling them. They see this as part of their delivery process and part of their job. And they're more successful because of it.

They target their knowledge acquisition like an athlete develops a training program. They look for gaps in skills and capabilities that, when filled, will increase output and provide the greatest return. They then aggressively fill those knowledge gaps through learning. Deliberate learners actively learn *and* strategically prioritize their learning.

Learning for learning's sake is great if you have the time. Otherwise, you have to be smart with your learning process and be very specific in what you learn and how and when you learn it. Use the rest of this chapter to scaffold your success in the information age.

DEVELOP A *MASTERY ORIENTATION*

A decade's worth of compelling research supports what I'm saying here. Researchers Carol Dweck at the University of Illinois and Ellen Leggett at Harvard University published their seminal work on deliberate learning in 1988, or to use their term, "mastery orientation."

Dweck and Legget put goal-setting under a microscope. They wanted to know if the type of goals we set and how we perceive those goals had an effect on our probability of achieving those goals. Their objective was to determine if some goal types were better than others.

Dweck and Leggett identified two types of goals: performance goals and learning goals. Performance goals are those in which the individuals setting them are concerned with gaining favorable judgment of their competence (think a four-minute mile or six hundred home runs). Learning goals are concerned with increasing competence (think learning how to hit a curve ball or learning how to hit a two-handed backhand in tennis).

In other words, those chasing performance goals are looking to establish the adequacy of their ability. They see goals as tests or measures of competence, which is almost always the case. When we see people exceed a goal, as in athletes setting records, we judge these people as the best. In sports, performance goals are exact measures of competence. In contrast, people who pursue learning goals, or mastery-oriented goals, tend to see achievement as learning opportunities—that is, they see learning goals as a way to acquire new skills and enhance their competency.

Dweck and Leggett's research found that there is a very clear association between the perception of the goals people set for themselves (performance versus learning) and the behaviors they employ to achieve them.

When the bar is low, it turns out that there is little difference between performance and learning goals in terms of behavior and achievement, so long as the goal is easy, requires little strategy, and lacks challenge. But when the bar is high, as the effort required to achieve either type of goal becomes more complicated and more challenging, and as strategies fail, the behavioral differences between performance goals and learning goals become stark.

In the face of difficulty and failure, those pursuing performance goals became negative and second-guessed their ability, and their performance rapidly declined. Performance goals become self-reinforcing. Success in a goal suggested, "I'm capable and good," whereas failure or difficulty suggested, "I suck, and I don't have the ability." When challenge and failure crept in, those pursuing performance goals crumbled like crumb cake.

On the other hand, those pursuing learning goals and those with a "mastery orientation" saw difficulty and failure as an opportunity to learn. They didn't blame or come up with excuses. Even more striking is that mastery-oriented people pursuing learning goals didn't see themselves as failing. They didn't see challenges and failures as a reflection on themselves or their ability. They viewed unsolved problems as challenges to be mastered through effort. Those pursuing learning goals engaged in extensive solution-oriented self-instruction and self-monitoring. Most importantly, mastery-oriented people in the pursuit of learning goals maintained tremendous optimism that in the end their efforts would pay off.

And you can bet their efforts did pay off! In the face of challenges, difficulties, and failure, those pursuing learning goals can expect increased goal attainment over those pursuing performance only. That's why learning on purpose—deliberate learning with a mastery orientation—is paramount to success.

Learn about Your Industry / Field

In the late 1990s and early 2000s, before the Internet became what it is now, I made a commitment to read a book a month. Trust me, that was a big deal for me back then. I was in my late twenties, early thirties. I was partying, traveling, playing, and living the life. Pinning myself down to read regularly was a big commitment.

It paid off, though. My career growth was meteoric during that period, and I owe much of it to my commitment to learn everything I could about sales, selling, business, leadership, and execution. The lessons from books I read back then still sit with me fifteen years later.

No matter what field you are in, I promise it's changing every day in the information age. If you're in sales, there are a millions sales approaches, tools, software applications, methodologies, and more about which you don't know. If you're in technology or coding specifically, I promise there are new coding frameworks, objects, languages, and so on about which you don't know. If you're in leadership, the learning opportunities about how to better lead your team are endless, almost infinite.

There is no field or profession today where committed deliberate learning can't help you. If you simply commit to a learning plan in your industry or field, the rewards will be exponential. Take the time to evaluate your knowledge gap in your industry, field, and profession, and build a deliberate learning plan to fill it. The key is to master the skills so you can go beyond being an expert and become a master.

COMMIT TO LEARNING ABOUT "YOU" AND BECOME A STUDENT OF YOU AND FOR YOU

We spend so much time with ourselves that it's common for us to lose sight of who we are and our strengths and weaknesses. I'm talking about self-awareness. Spending time learning about ourselves will improve our effectiveness. It's important to understand who we are and how we respond to stress, uncomfortable situations, other personalities, risk, certain environments, and more.

When we don't have an accurate understanding of who we are, we are not operating optimally. In fact, our efforts could be working against our goals.

Who we are is not a mystery. With few exceptions, everything about us is known by us or by others or both. This concept is best illustrated by the Johari window, which contrasts what we know about ourselves with what others know about us.

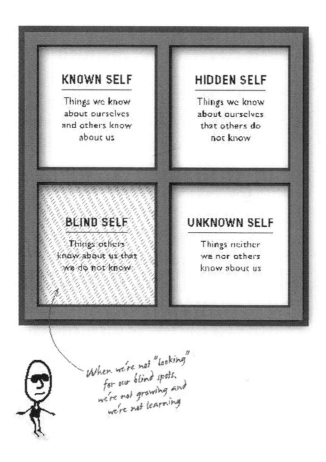

KNOWN SELF

Things we know about ourselves and others know about us

HIDDEN SELF

Things we know about ourselves that others do not know

BLIND SELF

Things others know about us that we do not know

UNKNOWN SELF

Things neither we nor others know about us

When we're not "looking" for our blind spots, we're not growing and we're not learning

What affects us most is our blind spot. When we are not self-aware, our blind spot/self grows. It's that part of us that we are unaware of that the rest of the world sees. Maybe you don't see yourself as abrasive, but the rest of the world does. Maybe you don't see yourself as demeaning, but the rest of the world does. Maybe you see yourself as a hard worker, but the rest of the world sees you as someone who just does enough to get by.

When our blind spot gets too big, our effectiveness shrinks. Our own behaviors and perspectives obstruct our ability to deliver. By committing to learning about the self, we minimize our blind spots. We become more self-aware and are able to focus on mastery goals that improve our effectiveness and our ability to be successful.

You are the vessel to success. The less you know about that vessel, the more difficult it is to sail.

Learn about Your Environment and Its People

- Do you know your neighbor four houses down on either side of you?
- What do you know about the sales department, the finance department, or HR?
- What do you know about the career aspirations of those who report to you?
- What do you know about the personal lives of your coworkers?
- What do you know about the sales guy at the competition?

- What do you know about the CEO at your biggest vendor?

If you're like most people, you probably don't know too much. We live, work, and play in massive environments and ecosystems about which we know very little. We move through our day-to-day lives, paying little mind to what's around us.

Learning about the world around us is key to our success in it. The world is too connected not to understand it. Information on people and companies is just as available as all other types of information. The Internet is packed with people's opinions and information about others.

Want to know about your biggest sales nemesis at the competition? LinkedIn can tell you almost all you need to know about her. You can find out what others think by reading their recommendations of her work. You can see the skills for which people recommend her, where she went to school, who she's connected to, the companies she follows, and groups to which she belongs and what she says in those groups. In many cases, you can also learn about her via her Instagram, Twitter, and even Facebook accounts.

Learning about people, companies, and the environments where we live and play is easy—*if* we are committed to learning about them. When we are familiar with the people and companies around us, we are better prepared to serve them or compete with them, whichever is your objective.

For most people, continuous, ongoing, self-directed, and deliberate learning was not part of the path to success. High school, college, and postgraduate educations acted as the primary learning paths. You could move up through the ranks by simply following the company-guided training and ongoing education, and by being a good company steward.

It's no longer enough to be a passive learner. Things move too fast. The problems are too complex and information is too readily available for us to not be deliberate learners. Success in the information age is going to come to those who see learning as a strategy, a way to exponentially increase their ability to deliver and to create change, innovate, and collaborate.

Like happiness, learning is a no-fail approach. When you learn, you always win.

CHAPTER 14

Bonus Skill: Be the Best You Can Be

WHEN I FINISHED this book, I still felt something was missing. I kept reading the thirteen skills and it didn't feel complete. I was missing something and couldn't figure it out.

Then I realized that I forgot about competition. I forgot that just doing these things isn't enough. You have to be really frickin' good at them. You have to be better at them than the next guy.

Here's one other thing that hasn't changed since the industrial age—competition. The competition for everything is just as fierce as it's always been. Competition is everywhere. Everyone is competing for the job you have or want. Every company is competing for customers. People are competing with you for venture capital money. They are competing with you for a spot on the team, a spot in the prestigious college, or that big promotion. That hot guy or gal in your office who you've been wanting to go out with? Yeah, that one. You're not the only one checking 'em out.

If you want to be successful in the twenty-first century, in addition to doing all the things in this book, you have to be a badass. You have to be the best you can absolutely be. You have to outperform everyone else who wants the same things you do. It's not enough just to do what's in this book if you can't be damn frickin' good.

Competition has only gotten more intense in the information age. As you've learned, there are more tools, more applications, more information, more access, more everything at your fingertips, and all of these changes have turned up the competitive heat.

If you want to win, if you want to be successful, you're gonna have to adopt these twenty-first century skills *and* bring your A game.

CHAPTER 15

WTF, Now What?

I KNOW THIS is a lot to take in.

In many cases, everything you've been taught has been tossed out the window. For those of us over forty and, worse, over fifty, these new rules to success are daunting. We've built our entire lives around our experience, not rocking the boat, working hard, keeping our heads down, and being good corporate stewards. We've gone to school and gotten our high school diplomas and college degrees, and some of us even earned advanced degrees. More people got their degrees in the past seventy-five years than in the history of man. We got more and more *experience*. We took fewer risks. We showed up on time and we worked hard. We did what we were told...and we were told that's how you climb the corporate ladder, that's how you become successful.

For many of us over forty, it's worked. Many achieved some semblance of success by executing the rules of the industrial age well. If you're lucky, you just might be able to sprint to the finish line without changing a thing. You may just be far enough along in your career that you can coast and ignore everything in this book. Congrats.

But if you're under forty or still looking to achieve greater success, then you're simply going to have to embrace these new skills. You're going to have to leverage the new skills that the information age is demanding. You're going to have to incorporate everything in this book. If you've been doing it the old way, you're going to have to work new muscles, focus on different things, and leave the old behind.

I'm not going to bullshit you. I got lucky. I wasn't some prognosticator who saw this coming. I didn't have some premonition; I simply saw a problem in my life and tried to solve it. No one told me that what it took to be successful was changing. I figured it out by accident, but I'm glad I did. It's changed everything in my life.

This book is meant to be a light switch. I wrote it to illuminate what many people aren't yet seeing and how that's having a substantial effect on their ability to achieve success. I've always loathed those people who move into a neighborhood and, once they're in, start passing laws or rules to keep others out. I'm not that kinda guy.

I get my kicks out of watching people be successful. I almost always cry at the end of *The Biggest Loser* because I see how happy these people are after losing all that weight. Their entire lives have opened up. I love seeing that happen to people. I'm sappy like that.

That's why I wrote this book. I want you to reach your goals, to achieve the success you want, no matter how you define it. And that's harder these days because no one is telling you that what it takes to be successful has changed. You haven't been taught—until now.

I get it. It's hard. Your natural reflexes are telling you that I'm crazy, that there's no way all these things are required for success. It's like bungee jumping. Even though you know you're attached to the bridge, your body is saying, "WTF! I'm not jumping off this fucking bridge. No, frickin' way." Unlike bungee jumping, however, you have to jump.

You have to jump into the information age.

Time stops for no one. The information age is waiting for no one. The importance of these skills is only going to increase over time and, without them, you'll just fall further and further behind.

The good news is that the core keys to success are still required. If you work your ass off leveraging these

141

new skills, if you have grit and are determined to kill it in these areas, and if you are passionate about what you do, look out. You'll be hypersuccessful with more options, relationships, and opportunities than you could have *ever* imagined.

Don't wait another second. Put this book down and start. Set your goals, build a plan, and go get it. If you don't, someone else will...they already are.

This isn't the end, only the beginning. We're gonna rock! I'm here for you. You can follow me on Twitter at @keenan and @nottaughtbook. I'm constantly dropping crazy 411 and mad insight on how to execute the things in this book. Let's get it on!

Here's to the gritty, hardworking, passionate ones.
May this book be your jet fuel.

Thought Leaders and Geniuses – Resources to Get It Done!

Learn how to master the skills in this
book from the masters themselves.

As I've said, the skills and ideas in this book aren't new. There are a lot of pioneers who have been out front, executing with brilliance and passion. They have perfected many of these skills for their own gain and the benefit of others. These people and companies have blazed our path into the information age.

To help you go deeper and get as much out of this book as possible, I've listed solid resources for each of the key skill sets. They will decrease your learning curve and accelerate your adoption and effectiveness. Why go it alone when you don't have to?

Where available, I've included Twitter handles, links, blogs, and books. Get following these people. You'll owe your success to them.

REACH

CHRIS BROGAN

Chris is a straight-up stud. He started his blog in 1998, and he's been ahead of the curve since the very beginning. Chris has built one of the most impressive and respected online brands. His website and books have helped countless people build powerful brands and launch successful small businesses. Brogan is a cornucopia of Internet branding and support. You need to check out all of his stuff.

Books:	*Trust Agents, The Freaks Shall Inherit the Earth*
Blog:	ChrisBrogan.com
Twitter:	@chrisbrogan

GARY VAYNERCHUK

Gary Vaynerchuk is a hustler. He moves at a hundred miles an hour and often talks about his nineteen-hour workdays. After getting out of college, Gary helped take his family's wine business from $3 million to $60 million in five years by leveraging social media to expand his reach. If there is a modern-day pioneer of reach, Gary Vee is it. Like Chris,

Gary is a must-follow for becoming a master of reach. His YouTube channel is likewise a must-watch.

Books: *Jab, Jab, Right Hook; Crush It; The Thank You Economy*
YouTube: Gary Vaynerchuk
Website: GaryVaynerchuk.com
Twitter: @garyvee

Brand You

Mark Fidelman

Mark is a quintessential salesman and branding expert. He's built an impressive brand himself. Mark is the CEO of Evolve, a marketing company. He's also a *Forbes* columnist, a *Huffington Post* columnist, and author. Mark's online training course for personal branding will set you up big! It's a must-watch.

Book: *Socialized*
Training: The Ultimate Guide to Building a Personal Brand
Twitter: @markfidelman

Dan Schawbel

Dan has literally written the book on personal branding, particularly for millennials and Gen Y. Dan Schawbel is the founder of WorkplaceTrends.com, a research and advisory membership service for forward-thinking HR professionals, as well as the managing partner of Millennial Branding, a Gen Y research and consulting firm. Dan is a best-selling author and thought leader whose work regularly appears in multiple media outlets.

Books: *Promote Yourself, Me 2.0*
Website: DanSchawbel.com
Twitter: @danschawbel

SHAMA HYDER

Known as the "Zen Master of Marketing" by Entrepreneur Magazine and the "Millennial Master of the Universe" by Fast Company, Shama Hyder is a visionary strategist for the digital age. When she isn't busy running her award-winning web marketing and digital PR firm, The Marketing Zen Group, she can be found writing books (her latest, *Momentum*, comes out in 2016), speaking at conferences alongside the world's top leaders (including President Obama and the Dalai Lama), or in the studio recording Shama.Tv. All in all, it explains why Forbes chose her for their 30 under 30 movers and shakers list for 2015. She is also a hot chocolate connoisseur, a Texan, and a Taurean.

Books: *The Zen of Social Media Marketing*
Website: http://www.marketingzen.com
Twitter: @shama

BRAND YOURSELF

Do you know what a Google search returns about you? Is it accurate? Are you showing up on the first page?

BrandYourself.com is a website that helps you improve your Google rankings. Get control of your Google search results.

CREATE CONTENT

DARREN ROWSE

Darren is the ProBlogger. You need to check out his stuff. Here's a bit of his story:

Back in 2002 I stumbled upon an article about "Blogging." I didn't know it at the time but that moment changed my life. I know that statements like that belong on those cheesy "buy my $1,000 training program" sites (don't worry I'm not selling anything more than a book) but it is actually true.

Within 24 hours of reading the article I had started my own Blog…I have slowly built my blogging into an income source that has enabled me to dedicate more and more time to the medium to the point where I am currently a full time blogger—a ProBlogger.

Book: *ProBlogger Book*
Blog: ProBlogger.net
Twitter: @problogger

ANN HANDLEY

Ann Handley speaks and writes about how you can re-think the way your business markets. Cited in *Forbes* as the most influential woman in social media and recognized by

ForbesWoman as one of the top twenty women bloggers, Ann Handley is the chief content officer of MarketingProfs, a training and education company with the largest community of marketers in its category.

Books: *Everybody Writes, Content Rules*
Blog: AnnHandley.com
Twitter: @marketingprofs

THINK

CLAUDIA ALTUCHER

Claudia Azula Altucher is a writer, podcast host, and teacher of yoga. She is the coauthor of the *Wall Street Journal* bestselling book *The Power of No* and author of *Become An Idea Machine* as well as *21 Things to Know Before Starting an Ashtanga Yoga Practice*.

Her writing has appeared in media outlets including *The New York Observer, Thought Catalog, Mantra Yoga +Health*, and *Positively Positive*. Claudia's book is more than a book but offers exercises for the mind. It provides a way to improve your ability to come up with new and powerful ideas. Can you come up with ten new ideas a day? It's time to try.

Book: *Become an Idea Machine*
Blog: claudiayoga.com
Twitter: @claudiayoga

HOLACRACY

There is a movement happening in management and organizational development circles called Holacracy. Started by Brian Robertson, this methodology requires thinking more than ever before. Its entire thesis is built on the idea that the individual offers a lot more value in making decisions than a hierarchical boss. In organizational structures like Holacracy, thinking is paramount. There is no boss to tell you what to do. As Robertson elaborates, "In Holacracy, people have multiple roles, often on different teams, and those role descriptions are constantly updated by the team actually doing the work. This allows people a lot more freedom to express their creative talents, and the company can take advantage of those skills in a way it couldn't before."

Book: *Holacracy: The New Management System for a Rapidly Changing World*
Blog: About Holacracy
Twitter: @h1brian

ART MARKMAN

Art's research explores thinking. He has studied the way people form and use analogies, the mechanisms of decision-making, the modes that allow people to form categories, and the influences of motivation on reasoning. Art is also the executive editor of the journal *Cognitive Science* and is a former executive officer of the Cognitive Science Society.

Art Markman is the Annabel Irion Worsham Centennial Professor of Psychology and Marketing at the University of Texas at Austin. He is also the Founding Director of the Program in the Human Dimensions of Organizations. The HDO program brings the humanities and the social behavioral sciences to people in business.

Book: Smart Thinking Smart Change
Website: Smartthinkingbook.com
Twitter: @abmarkman

TIM HURSON

Throughout his career, Tim has helped Fortune 500 and FTSE 100 organizations in the US, Canada, and the UK create innovation, marketing, new product, and workplace transformation programs. In the process, he's seen how barriers to creative and productive thinking are also barriers to success — for individuals and for groups.

He speaks regularly about how to use the principles of productive thinking and creative leadership to manage change rather than be swamped by it. He shows how organizations can foster a creative working environment, stable enough to provide cultural continuity and flexible enough to adjust to rapid changes in technologies, markets, and mandates.

Book: *Think Better, Never Be Closing*
Website: TimHurson.com
Twitter: @tim_hurson

Screw Your Degree

Peter Thiel

"The Thiel Fellowship is unlike anything you've ever experienced. The Fellowship brings together some of the world's most creative and motivated young people, and helps them bring their most ambitious projects to life. Thiel Fellows are given a grant of $100,000 to focus on their work, their research, and their self-education while outside of university. Fellows are mentored by our community of visionary thinkers, investors, scientists, and entrepreneurs, who provide guidance and business connections that can't be replicated in any classroom. With tens of thousands in additional resources, summer housing, regular workshops, our Thiel Foundation Summits, fellowship dinners, and retreats we've built a robust community and program to accelerate your professional and personal development. Rather than just studying, you're doing."

Book: *Zero to One: Notes on Startups, or How to Build the Future*

Website: ThielFellowship.org

Twitter: @peterthiel

Change

Dan and Chip Heath

The Heath brothers' book, *Switch*, asks the following question: why is it so hard to make lasting changes in our companies, in our communities, and in our own lives? The primary obstacle, according to the Heaths, is a conflict that's built into our brains. Psychologists have discovered that our minds are ruled by two different systems—the rational mind and the emotional mind—that compete for control. The rational mind wants a great beach body; the emotional mind wants that Oreo cookie. The rational mind wants to change something at work; the emotional mind loves the comfort of the existing routine. This tension can doom a change effort—but if it is overcome, change can come quickly.

Book: *Switch*
Website: HeathBrothers.com

John Kotter

An authority on leadership and change, Dr. John P. Kotter is a *New York Times* best-selling author, award-winning business and management thought leader, business entrepreneur, inspirational speaker, and Harvard professor. His ideas and books, as well as his company Kotter International, have helped mobilize people around the world to better lead organizations and their own lives in an era of increasingly rapid change.

Books: *Our Iceberg Is Melting, Leading Change, Sense of Urgency*
Website: KotterInternational.com
Twitter: @johnpkotter

Spencer Johnson

Most people are fearful of change because they don't believe they have any control over how or when it happens to them. Since change happens either to the individual or by the individual, Spencer Johnson, author of *Who Moved My Cheese? An Amazing Way to Deal with Change in Your Work and in Your Life*, shows us that what matters most is the attitude we have about change.

Book: *Who Moved My Cheese?*
Website: SpencerJohnson.com

Time versus Results

Larry Bossidy and Ram Charan

Although a little dated, this book changed my life. It set me up perfectly to look at delivering results in an entirely new way. No one else had highlighted the importance and path to delivering results, beyond just doing work or working hard. *Execution* will be your Bible for getting results, I promise you. Larry Bossidy is one of the world's most acclaimed CEOs, a man with few peers who has a track record for delivering results. Ram Charan is a legendary adviser to senior executives and boards of directors, a man with unparalleled insight into why some companies are successful and others are not. Together they've pooled their knowledge and experience into the one book on how to close the gap between results promised and results delivered that people in business need today.

Book: *Execution*
LinkedIn: Ram Charan

Have the Balls to Make It Happen

Margie Warrell

Margie Warrell is an international thought leader in human potential who is passionate about empowering people live and lead more courageously. Margie draws on her professional background in Fortune 500 business, psychology, and coaching to provide programs on communication, leadership. and resilience to a diverse range of organizations worldwide. Her client list includes NASA, British Telecom, PWC, and the Australian Federal Police to name a few.

Books: *Stop Playing Safe, Brave, Find Your Courage*
Website: MargieWarrell.com
Twitter: @margiewarrell

Learn to Sell

Daniel Pink

Dan Pink is the author of five provocative books, including three long-running *New York Times* best sellers *A Whole New Mind*, *Drive*, and *To Sell Is Human*. His articles on business and technology appear in many publications, including the *New York Times*, *Harvard Business Review*, *Fast Company*, *Wired*, and *The Sunday Telegraph*. (See a sample of articles here.)

Book: *To Sell Is Human*

Website: DanielPink.com
Twitter: @danielpink

JILL KONRATH

Not only is Jill a personal friend of mine, she is a true badass in every way. She knows how to sell. She is the author
of three best-selling award-winning sales books. Her new-
est book, *Agile Selling*, shows salespeople how to succeed
in a constantly changing sales world. *S.N.A.P. Selling* focuses on what it takes to win sales with today's crazy-busy
buyers. And *Selling to Big Companies* provides step-by-step
guidance on setting up meetings with corporate decision
makers.

Book: *S.N.A.P. Selling, Agile Selling, Selling to Big*
         Companies
Website: JillKonrath.com
Twitter: @jillkonrath

KOKA SEXTON

Koka is the leader in social selling. Social selling is the
intersection between knowing how to sell, social media,
reach, and branding. It's the confluence of all four of these
crucial success traits. Ranked by *Forbes* as the number-one
social seller in the world, Koka is ahead of the selling curve
in the twenty-first century. Koka is LinkedIn's group
manager for content and social marketing, responsible for
LinkedIn's focus on content marketing for consumers and
helping them get the most out of LinkedIn. Koka is selling

in the information age, and following him will be one of the smartest things you can do.

LinkedIn: Koka Sexton
Twitter: @kokasexton

EXPERIENCE VERSUS EXPERTISE

THE DUNNING-KRUGER EFFECT

People tend to hold overly favorable views of their abilities in many social and intellectual domains. The authors suggest that this overestimation occurs in part because people who are unskilled in these domains suffer a dual burden. Not only do these people reach erroneous conclusions and make unfortunate choices, but their incompetence robs them of the metacognitive ability to realize it. Across four studies, the authors found that participants scoring in the bottom quartile on tests of humor, grammar, and logic grossly overestimated their test performance and ability. Although their test scores put them in the twelfth percentile, they estimated themselves to be in the sixty-second percentile. Several analyses linked this miscalibration to deficits in metacognitive skill, or the capacity to distinguish accuracy from error. This study might just give you a little bit of humility. If you've been counting your experience as justification of your expertise, you just may be unskilled and unaware. Get focused on growing and expanding your expertise, stop measuring in years, and start measuring in knowledge.

Study: "Unskilled and Unaware of It"
Twitter: @daviddunning6

HAVE FUN. BE HAPPY.

MARTIN SELIGMAN

Commonly known as the founder of positive psychology, Martin Seligman is a leading authority in the fields of positive psychology, resilience, learned helplessness, depression, optimism, and pessimism. He is also a recognized authority on interventions that prevent depression and build strengths and well-being.

Books: *Learned Optimism, Flourish*
Website: AuthenticHappiness.com
TED Talk: The New Era of Positive Psychology

RONALD CULBERSON

Through keynote presentations, seminars, and humor writing, Ron Culberson's mission is change the workplace culture so that organizations are more productive and staff are more content.

Books: Do It Well. Make It Fun; Is Your Glass Laugh Full?
Website: RonCulberson.com
Twitter: @ronculberson

GRETCHEN RUBIN

Gretchen Rubin is the author of several books, including the blockbuster *New York Times* bestsellers *Better Than Before*, *The Happiness Project*, and *Happier at Home*. She has an enormous readership, both in print and online, and her books have sold more than two million copies worldwide, in more than thirty languages. On her weekly podcast, *Happier with Gretchen Rubin*, she discusses good habits and happiness with her sister Elizabeth Craft. The podcast hit number-six on iTunes on the first day it launched. It ranks in the top 1 percent of podcasts and has listeners in more than 192 countries.

Book: *The Happiness Project*
Website: GretchenRubin.com
Twitter: @gretchenrubin

SONJA LYUMBOMIRSKY

The majority of my research career has been devoted to studying human happiness. Why is the scientific study of happiness important? In short, because most people believe happiness is meaningful, desirable, and an important, worthy goal, because happiness is one of the most salient and significant dimensions of human experience and emotional life, because happiness yields numerous rewards for the individual, and because it makes for a better, healthier, stronger society. Along these lines, my current research addresses three critical questions – 1) What makes people happy?; 2) Is happiness a good thing?; and 3) How can we make people happier still?

Books:	*The How of Happiness*, *The Myths of Happiness*
Website:	SonjaLyubomirsky.com
Twitter:	@slyubomirsky

DON'T BE BORING

VANESSA VAN EDWARDS

Vanessa is a recovering boring person. She is a published author and behavioral investigator, and a professional people watcher—speaking, researching, and cracking the code of interesting human behavior for audiences around the world. Vanessa's groundbreaking workshops and courses teach individuals how to succeed in business and life by understanding the hidden dynamics of people. Vanessa is a *Huffington Post* columnist and Penguin author. She has been featured on many other media outlets.

Website:	ScienceofPeople.com
Twitter:	@vvanedwards

DELIBERATE LEARNING

MAURICE GIBBONS

A specialist in the creation of innovative approaches to instruction, the programs he has designed emphasize self-direction, challenge and excellence. In 2007, Gibbon's was awarded the *Malcolm Knowles Memorial Self Directed Learning Award* at the 21st annual International Self Directed Learning Symposium. Maurice is a Canadian who grew up on the west coast, completed his BA at the University of British Columbia, his MA in English at the University of Washington, and his doctorate at Harvard where he was on the editorial board of the Harvard Educational Review.

Website: www.selfdirectedlearning.com

Peace, I'm Out!

Made in the USA
San Bernardino, CA
07 May 2018